ON WRITING AND POLITICS

Günter Grass

ON WRITING
AND POLITICS
1967-1983

Translated by Ralph Manheim

Introduction by Salman Rushdie

A Helen and Kurt Wolff Book

A Harvest/HBJ Book

Harcourt Brace Jovanovich, Publishers
SAN DIEGO   NEW YORK   LONDON

Library of Congress Cataloging in Publication Data
Grass, Günter, 1927–
   On writing and politics, 1967–1983.
   "Helen and Kurt Wolff book."
   1. Grass, Günter, 1927– —Political and social views—Addresses, essays, lectures.
2. Grass, Günter, 1927– —Knowledge—Literature—Addresses, essays, lectures.
3. German literature—20th century—History and criticism—Addresses, essays,
lectures. I. Title.
PT2613.R338A25 1985   838'.91409   85-786
ISBN 0-15-169969-0
ISBN 0-15-668793-3 (Harvest/HBJ : pbk.)

Designed by Margaret M. Wagner
Printed in the United States of America
First Harvest/HBJ edition 1986
A B C D E F G H I J

CONTENTS

INTRODUCTION

In the summer of 1967, when the West was—perhaps for the last time—in the clutches of the optimism disease, when the microscopic, invisible bacilli of optimism made its young people believe that they would overcome some day, when unemployment was an irrelevance and the future still existed, and when I was twenty years old, I bought a paperback copy of Ralph Manheim's English translation of *The Tin Drum* from a bookshop in Cambridge, England. In those days everybody had better things to do than read. There was the music and there were the movies and there was also, don't forget, the world to change. Like many of my contemporaries I spent my student years under the spell of Buñuel, Godard, Ray, Wajda, Welles, Bergman, Kurosawa, Jancsó, Antonioni, Dylan, Lennon, Jagger, Laing, Marcuse and, inevitably, the two-headed fellow known to Grass readers as Marxengels. In spite of all these distractions, however, Oskar Matzerath's autobiography had me hooked, and I stayed hooked all the way from grandmother Anna Koljaiczek's wide skirt, past fizz powder and horse's head full of eels, right up to Anna's dark opposite, the wicked Black Witch.

There are books that open doors for their readers, doors in the head, doors whose existence they had not previously suspected. And then there are readers who dream of becoming writers; they are searching for the strangest door of all, scheming up ways to travel through the page, to end up inside and also behind the writing, to lurk between the lines while other readers, in their turn, pick up books and begin to dream. For these Alices, these would-be migrants from the World to the Book, there are (if they are lucky) books which give them permission to travel, so to speak, permission to become the sort of writers they have it in themselves to be. A passport is a kind of book. And my passports, the works that gave me the permits I needed, were *The Film Sense* by Sergei Eisenstein, the *Crow* poems of Ted Hughes, Borges's *Fictions*, Sterne's *Tristram Shandy*, Ionesco's play *Rhinoceros*—and, that summer of 1967, *The Tin Drum*.

This is what Grass's great novel said to me in its drumbeats: Go for broke. Always try and do too much. Dispense with safety nets. Take a deep breath before you begin talking. Aim for the stars. Keep grinning. Be ruthless. Argue with the world. And never forget that writing is as close as we get to keeping a hold on the thousand and one things—childhood, certainties, cities, doubts, dreams, instants, phrases, parents, loves—that go on slipping, like sand, through our fingers. I have tried to learn the lessons of the midget drummer. And one more, which I got from that other, immense work, *Dog Years*: When you've done it once, start all over again and do it better.

Günter Grass, Danzig's most famous son (Lech Walesa, the only other contender for the title, inhabits—it's important to insist —not Danzig but Gdansk), Günter Grass who now lives partly in Berlin, a city which itself seems to have migrated to a new and starker location, and partly in a North German landscape which reminds him of the wide, diked vistas of his writing and his youth, is a figure of central importance in the literature of migration, and the migrant is, perhaps, the central or defining figure of the twentieth century. And like many migrants, like many people who have lost a city, he has found it in his luggage, packed in an old tin box. Kundera's Prague, Joyce's Dublin, Grass's Danzig: exiles, refugees, migrants have carried many cities in their bedrolls in this century of wandering. And let nobody underestimate the obstinacy of such writers; they will not tolerate the Gdansking of their past. In Grass's transported city, Labesweg is still Labesweg and the shipyard which saw the birth of Solidarity is not called Lenin but Schichau. (Here, once again, I feel a small affinity. I grew up on Warden Road, Bombay; now it's Bhulabhai Desai Road. I went to school near Flora Fountain; now the school is near Hutatma Chowk. Of course the new, decolonized names tell of a confident, assertive spirit in the independent state; but the loss of past attachments remains a loss. What to do? Shrug. And pickle the past in books.)

In one sense, Grass is only approximately half a migrant. A full migrant suffers, traditionally, a triple disruption: he loses his place, he enters into an alien language, and he finds himself surrounded by beings whose social behavior and code is very unlike, and sometimes even offensive to, his own. And this is what makes migrants such important figures: because roots, language and social norms have been three of the most important parts of the definition of what it is to be a human being. The migrant, denied all three, is obliged to find new ways of describing himself, new ways of being human.

Well, Grass certainly lost his place (and, as I suggested, found that he'd brought it along with him). It's possible to argue that he lost a part of his language, the Kashubian dialects of his youth which he attempted to preserve in his writing; but here I'm on thin ice, as my knowledge of German is probably about as great as Grass's knowledge of Urdu. At any rate, apart from the dialects, it seems difficult to suggest that Grass is a writer out of language, and certainly he has remained within a society whose social mores are known to him. Indeed, as his essays show, his dedication to the idea of a German civilization which embraces both West and East Germany and which finds its true expression in the German language, is complete. One may therefore legitimately ask how useful this notion of a half-migrant Grass, a maybe-only-one-third-migrant Grass, really is.

I think it is useful, because there are other senses in which Grass seems to me to be very much more than merely a frag-

Introduction

ment or percentage of a migrant writer. Migration across national frontiers is by no means the only form of the phenome-
non. In many ways, given the international and increasingly
homogeneous nature of metropolitan culture, the journey from,
for example, rural America to New York City is a more extreme
act of migration than a move from, say, Bombay. But I want to
go further than such literalistic discussions; because migration
also offers us one of the richest metaphors of our age. The very
word *metaphor*, with its roots in the Greek words for *bearing
across*, describes a sort of migration, the migration of ideas into
images. Migrants—borne-across humans—are metaphorical beings in their very essence; and migration, seen as a metaphor,
is everywhere around us. We all cross frontiers; in that sense,
we are all migrant peoples.

Günter Grass is a migrant from his past, and now I am no
longer talking about Danzig. He grew up, as he has said, in a
house and a milieu in which the Nazi view of the world was
treated quite simply as objective reality. Only when the Americans came at the war's end and the young Grass began to hear
how things had really been in Germany did he understand that
the lies and distortions of the Nazis were not the plain truth.
What an experience: to discover that one's entire picture of the
world is false, and not only false, but based upon a monstrosity.
What a task for any individual: the reconstruction of reality
from rubble.

I am suggesting that we can see this process as an act of
migration, from an old self into a new one. That the end of
World War II was for Grass, as it was for Germany, as tough
and disrupting a frontier to cross as any one can imagine. And
if we call Grass a migrant of this type, we quickly discover that
the triple dislocation classically suffered by migrants has indeed
been in operation in the case of Migrant Grass, the man who
migrated across history. The first dislocation, remember, is the
loss of roots. And Grass lost not only Danzig; he lost—he must
have lost—the sense of home as a safe, "good" place. How could
it retain that feeling in the light of what he learned about it at

the war's end? The second dislocation is linguistic. And we know—and Grass has written often and eloquently—of the effect of the Nazi period on the German language, of the need for the language to be rebuilt, pebble by pebble, from the wreckage; because a language in which evil finds so expressive a voice is a dangerous tongue. The practitioners of "rubble literature"—Grass himself being one of the most prominent of these—took upon themselves the Herculean task of re-inventing the German language, of tearing it apart, ripping out the poisoned parts, and putting it back together.

And the third disruption is social. Once again we can argue that the transformation in German society, or, rather, in the Germany that the growing Grass knew and experienced, was of the same order as the change in social codes that a migrant from one country to another experiences: that Nazi Germany was, in some ways, another country. Grass had to unlearn that country, that way of thinking about society, and learn a new one.

I see Grass, then, as a double migrant: a traveler across borders in the self, and in Time. And the vision underlying his writing, both fiction and nonfiction, is, I believe, in many ways a migrant's vision.

This is what the triple disruption of reality teaches migrants: that reality is an artifact, that it does not exist until it is made, and that, like any other artifact, it can be made well or badly, and that it can also, of course, be unmade. What Grass learned on his journey across the frontiers of history was Doubt. Now he distrusts all those who claim to possess absolute forms of knowledge; he suspects all total explanations, all systems of thought which purport to be complete. Amongst the world's great writers, he is quintessentially the artist of uncertainty, whose symbol might easily have been the question mark if it were not the Snail. To experience any form of migration is to get a lesson in the importance of tolerating others' points of view. One might almost say that migration ought to be essential training for all would-be democrats.

About that Snail. This social-democratic mollusk, under whose spiraling shell are housed the ideas of hurrying slowly, caution, circumspection, and gradualism, has served Grass well, and also earned him his share of brickbats from those who advocate more rapid rates of advance. I don't want to enter that dispute here, noting only that there are times—for instance during his advocacy of nuclear disarmament—when Grass himself appears far from Snailesque. But I should like to use the Snail as evidence that Grass lives more comfortably in images, in ideas, than in places. This, too, is a characteristic of migrants. He is, after all, a metaphorical being.

The migrant intellect roots itself in itself, in its own capacity for imagining and re-imagining the world. This can lead to difficulties: is it because the United States is a migrants' culture that its citizens can, at times (election campaigns, for instance), appear to prefer image to substance? But the love of images also contains great potential. When the world is seen through ideas, through metaphors, it becomes a richer place. When Grass looks at Czechoslovakia through the writing of Kafka, or contemporary Japanese urban sprawl through the images of Alfred Döblin, he helps us see more, and more clearly.

A writer who understands the artificial nature of reality is more or less obliged to enter the process of making it. This is perhaps why Grass has so determinedly sought a public role, why he has used his great fame as a novelist as a platform from which to speak on the many issues—the bomb, the invasion of our privacy by data banks, the relationship between the nations of the rich North and the poor South—which concern him. And since to argue about reality is to be at once creative and political, it is not surprising that when Grass writes about literature he finds himself writing about politics, and when he discusses political issues, the quirky perspectives of literature have a habit of creeping in.

In his essay "The Destruction of Mankind Has Begun" Grass makes the telling point that, for the first time in the history of the species, writers can no longer assume the existence of posterity. He says that, as a result, "the book I am planning to write . . . will have to include a farewell to the damaged world, to wounded creatures, to us and our minds, which have thought of everything and the end as well." And the composition of elegies is indeed one of the proper responses for a writer to make when night is drawing in. But outside his fiction, in his political activities and writings, Grass is also making a second, and equally proper, response. What this work says is: We aren't dead yet. We may be in deep trouble but we aren't done for. And while there is life, there must be analysis, struggle, persuasion, argument, polemic, rethinking, and all the other longish words that add up to one very short word: hope.

—Salman Rushdie

On Writing

DÖBLIN, MY TEACHER

First published in Akzente, *14 (1967).*

I never saw him and this is how I imagine him: small, nervous, jumpy, nearsighted and for that reason bent close to reality; a visionary given to shorthand, the pressure of whose ideas leaves him no time to construct careful periods. With each new book he starts all over again, refutes himself and his changing theories. Manifestoes, articles, books, ideas tread on one another's heels, a chaotic crowd: where is the author?

When we speak of Alfred Döblin today—if we speak of him at all—we speak mostly of *Berlin Alexanderplatz.* There are reasons for this simplification of a writer whom I would like to set beside—and against—Thomas Mann, beside and against Bertolt Brecht; there are reasons for this exclusive concentration on a single one of his works. Thomas Mann, and to an even greater extent Bertolt Brecht, consciously fitted their work into a classical mold, which they themselves devised and worked out in detail. Verifiably, and not without references to a classical tradition prolonged by themselves, these authors set stone after stone upon a clearly circumscribed base. And even when Brecht tried, with a play like *The Measures Taken,* to throw his plan overboard, he gave up quickly enough to enable later interpreters to gloss over this breakaway phase.

The secondary literature about both these authors fills shelf upon shelf. Soon Brecht, like Kafka, will be interpreted away from us. Alfred Döblin has been spared such abduction to the Empyrean. This anticlassical writer has never had a school, not even a school of enemies. The edition of his collected works, published by Walter Verlag and edited by Walter Muschg, is gathering dust on the publisher's shelves.

Whole generations have "simply" grown up with Thomas Mann; the moment we run into some little snag with bureaucratic institutions, the word "Kafkaesque" springs to our lips; our Brecht buffs can be recognized by their participial constructions; only Alfred Döblin moves no congresses, seldom fires the industry of our Germanists, seduces few readers. Even his famous *Berlin Alexanderplatz* has never succeeded in celebrating a homecoming in present-day Berlin; often as we may run into Franz Biberkopf in various corner saloons, and much as that occasional hawker of nationalist newspapers might today be tempted to peddle the *Morgenpost*, he has never got out of East Berlin.

For this reason I beg leave to set Mann, Brecht, and Kafka respectfully aside, despite the long shadow cast by their much-cited greatness, and as a pupil express my gratitude to my teacher. For I owe Alfred Döblin a lot; indeed, I cannot conceive of my prose without the futuristic component of such of his books as *Wang-Lun; Wallenstein; Mountains, Oceans, and Giants*; and *Berlin Alexanderplatz*. In other words, since writers are never self-generated, but come from somewhere, I wish to say that I come from this Döblin, who before coming from Kierkegaard came from Charles de Coster, whose parenthood he acknowledged in writing his *Wallenstein*.

Wallenstein is no more a historical novel than is *Thyl Ulenspiegel*. Döblin regards history as an absurd process. No Hegelian *Weltgeist* rides across battlefields for him. His heroes in the battle against absurdity—whether Franz Biberkopf in *Berlin Alexanderplatz* or Edward in his *Hamlet* novel—have one thing in common with de Coster's Thyl, their "forthrightness," though little of this can be detected in *Wallenstein*, the epic directly influenced by de Coster. In *Wallenstein* the historical course of an exacerbated, visionary absurdity is traced so coldly that no author seems to be involved in it, and then is repeatedly smashed into bits.

But before we speak of *Wallenstein*, which should properly be titled "The Other Ferdinand," let's try to situate this book among Döblin's works.

In *Epilogue*, one of his last essays, Döblin deals with—or, rather, writes off—his work. Carelessly and impatiently, as though improvising, he lists his works and at the same time distances himself from them. He attaches importance only to his last book, *Hamlet, or The End of the Long Night*. He has turned Catholic, and with the unquestioning certitude of a Catholic convert he looks upon his own work as vanity. Having already turned away, he looks back: "Our vile spirit will not be quieted. . . . Satan walks among us." For him, the visionary of reason, the cool, disinterested observer of driven masses and contradictory realities, the recorder of simultaneous movements that impeded and annulled one another, the utopian builder of worlds who painted the deglaciation of Greenland on a wide canvas, the hour of faith had struck. I can follow him no longer.

The refugee Döblin reads Kierkegaard at the Bibliothèque Nationale and, irresistibly, becomes first a Christian, then a Catholic. Another man reads, say, the Bible and becomes a Marxist. At the age of fourteen, when I read *Crime and Punishment*, I understood nothing and understood too much. The usual fruits of reading? Not really. I see books more as time bombs: once detached from the author, they explode in the reader's head. But since we can assume that Döblin had always kept his fuse in readiness so that some day, while (as lonely as one can only be at the Bibliothèque Nationale in Paris) he was looking for atlases and travel books, the detonator Kierkegaard might come along, we can at least guess at the often long-delayed effect books can have. For we know little about the effect of books. And still less does the author know what soil his word will fall on.

On the one hand, a man who listens pragmatically to ordinary speech, who (especially in *Berlin Alexanderplatz*) lets spoken dialogue compete with his inner monologue; and, on the other hand, a man with an inventive mind whose visions and apocalypses are always on the lookout for mystical ecstasy. Where is the author? A picture puzzle. Should we look for him in the jungles of a Jesuit state in Amazonia, in the Berlin slaughterhouse, or prostrate before an altar of Our Lady, the pagan design of which reminds us of Veneska, the Queen Mother of a utopian troubadour empire after the deglaciation of Greenland?

This much is certain: Döblin knew that a book has to be more than its author, that the author is only a means to an end—that is, the book—and that an author must cultivate hiding places, which he leaves to speak his manifesto and seeks out to take refuge behind a book.

Döblin's *Epilogue* begins like this: "A pile of books is lying here. . . ." "Here" is the wrong word; it should be "A pile of books exists; they were written over a period of five decades; here they are not."

After a number of Early Expressionist stories, later collected in the volume *The Murder of a Buttercup*, he published in 1912 his first novel, *Wang-Lun's Three Leaps*. He was instantly and immediately "here," though without immediate success.

Wang-Lun, the leader of the weak and defenseless, becomes culpable by trying to give weakness the status of an ideology. The atrocities committed by the drop-outs and weaklings of the Manchu era are comparable to the atrocities of the powerful; Wang-Lun, the gentle berserker, fails and kills himself. But close as this thesis is to the best German Kohlhaas and Karl Moor tradition,* the language is new, despite its ornamental ties with the Jugendstil, and the treatment of crowd scenes is stunningly revolutionary. Once set in motion, the people storm

---

*Michael Kohlhaas (in Heinrich von Kleist's novel by that name) and Karl Moor (in Friedrich Schiller's early play *Die Räuber*) are led to criminal violence by an exacerbated desire for justice. —ED.

mountains, become a moving mountain; the elements join in their assault. With *Wang-Lun's Three Leaps* Döblin gave us the first futurist novel.

From then on the Expressionists around Walden, Hille, and Stramm have regarded him as a renegade, and in his *Open Letter to Marinetti*, Döblin, who thought well of futurist painting, broke with the futurist writers as well. He had seen eye to eye with them, he said, as long as their aim was to get closer to reality; but Marinetti reduced reality to technology, to the mere world of machines. Döblin was against categorical ukases, against the monomaniacal amputation of syntax, against the mania for larding prose with images, analyses, and metaphors; Marinetti, he held, should learn to do without images; the prose writer's problem was to dispense with images. Literally: ". . . whether with or without periods is all the same to me. I refuse to listen fifty times to a lot of trum-trum, tatatata, etc., which requires no great command of the language. . . . I refuse to let theories cheat me out of the specific breathless reality of a battle. . . ."

This impassioned letter ends abruptly: "You to your futurism. I to my Döblinism."

A year later the self-assured doctor was himself trying his hand at categorical ukases. He issued his "Berlin program," sternly impugning those novelists who persist in "mulling over the problems of their own inadequacy." "Writing is not biting your nails or picking your teeth. It is a public activity."

"The subject matter of a novel," Döblin declared, "is untrammeled reality; a sovereignly independent reader is confronted with a fully formed sequence of events; it is up to him, not to the author, to judge."

Döblin demanded, excluded, issued rules. "Abundant use should be made of artfully structured sentences, which enable a writer to sum up quickly a complex juxtaposition and sequence of factors. Quick developments, confusion in bare catchwords; in general, a writer must aim at the utmost precision through suggestive turns of phrase. The whole must not make the impression of something spoken, but of something real and present."

In 1917, while Döblin was working on a manuscript intended to confirm some of his theories and break the bounds of confining rules, he continued his dogmatic theoretical work. The tenor is still exclusionary. In an essay entitled *Observations on the Novel*, he again marks out his self-imposed limits: "The novel has nothing to do with plot; we know that originally not even the drama had anything to do with it, and it is questionable whether the drama was well advised to take the rigid form it did. To simplify, pound, and carve reality into the shape of a plot is not the business of an epic writer. The novelist's watchword is 'Classify, accumulate, rearrange, and disarrange'; that of the present-day impoverished, plot-obsessed dramatist is 'Get ahead!' 'Get ahead' can never be the watchword of the novel."

Army Doctor Döblin wrote this analysis in the midst of the First World War. The mutilated of Verdun were channeled into the hospitals of Alsace and Lorraine. While the battle of the armaments industries was teaching what progress means in warfare, Dr. Döblin, in what free time his patients left him, immersed himself in documents relating to the Thirty Years' War. Though at first those remote years meant nothing more to him than an incredible number of battles among factions he found it almost impossible to keep apart and remember, he soon began to classify, accumulate, rearrange, and disarrange chronicles and documents, paper distillations of history. In *Epilogue* he wrote, thirty years later, "I wallowed in facts. I was in love, fascinated by these records and reports. I'd have liked best to use them just as they were." But in the beginning, before the magic of documents had transported him to another century—or, as in *Wang-Lun*, to China, which was known to him only from atlases—before this immersion there came his all-sustaining idea, the epic vision that struck the spark.

In the previous year, poor health had sent Army Doctor Döblin to Bad Kissingen for a cure. An item in the newspaper, the announcement of a Gustavus Adolphus festival play, had released the mechanism. There he sits, a small, restless, near-sighted man, under the trees of the casino park. He sees the Baltic, sees the cogs and corvettes sailing on and on, sees Gustavus Adolphus coming from Sweden with his fleet.

With clattering yards the swiftly moving ships, swollen sailing vessels throwing out their chests, emerge from the dripping water, still nameless, still coming from nowhere. Sweden is still obscure; it hasn't arrived yet and hasn't yet acquired a political destiny; it's just a glide through the seas, a conquest of space, which drives the present reality of Verdun from the mind of an army doctor who has come to Bad Kissingen to convalesce.

Soon this vision will be given a title. *Andromeda, Rainbow, Stork, Dolphin, Parrot, Black Dog* are the names of the ships. The flagship, the *Mercury,* is armed with thirty-two guns. The men come from Svealand and Gotland, from Finland, land of lakes. They put ashore near Wolgast in Pomerania.

The vision that came floating to Army Doctor Döblin through the trees of the casino park has now found its place; actually, measured by the overall plan, it has contracted. For the space of a page, the Swedish fleet is allowed, in crossing the Baltic Sea, to ring in the beginning of book five, but its grandly synchronized movement is imparted to the whole epic. The one single-minded event, here hinted at with the first sentence of the section titled "Sweden"—"Over the waves of the gray-green Baltic, wind-driven, came the mighty fleet of the Swedes, cogs, galleons, corvettes"—is modulated in all its breadth from the beginning to the end of the six-part volume.

Wallenstein begins with the Emperor Ferdinand's victory banquet. This bacchanal, the numerous courses enriched with culinary or allegorical decorations, the hierarchy of guests wearing Spanish ruffs, jerkins laced in Hungarian green, French vests, purple cloaks, is an occasion for serving up here and there the defeat of Bohemia and of Frederick, the poor landless Count Palatine: "An abbot bit the leg off a capon and while cracking it inventoried the abandoned Palatine silver plate given him by pious Walloons in Bohemia." And with the dinner music, shortly before the cakes and jellies, the full-to-bursting cardinals, abbots, generals, and princes see the defeated army of the "magnificent curly-blond Frederick move through the hall, ride through the clatter and uproar of voices, cups, and dishes, down from the hanging carpet of the choir to the two flaming chandeliers, dash against the billowing curtain through which the marshals and their henchmen have stepped: magnificently hacked Palatine corpses, headless trunks, sightless eyes, carts, carts full of corpses, drawn by asses, swathed in dust and foulness, packed into crates that bob and sway like branches, gee up, gee up through the air."

Döblin has his own way of placing the accents: to him victories, defeats, treaties, all the dated facts that, taken together, have come to be known as the Thirty Years' War, are worth no more than a subordinate clause or are, often enough, deliberately passed over. What interests him is the comings and goings of the armies looking for winter quarters, the labyrinthine court intrigues, dragged through chancelleries, palace gardens, and hidden galleries, and ending up in confessionals. From barely moving lips he reads Jesuit whispers; rosaries and indulgences spark off history, the consequences of which he notes succinctly at the end. Distorted as by concave mirrors, mystically heightened, the tangled rituals of cunning preparation, spun in Vienna or at the court of Maximilian of Bavaria, roll over whole pages, while the outcome of courtiers' efforts, such as the deposition of Wallenstein or the refusal of the Elector of Saxony to let Gustavus Adolphus and his army pass through Saxon territory, are mentioned (without special emphasis) only because such things just happen to be part of the picture; but history they are not, for history means the innumerable absurd simultaneities that Döblin wants to lay bare.

The Thirty Years' War has been, and no doubt remains, a source and stimulant of German-language literature. The German novel can be said to begin with *Simplicissimus*. Like Döblin after him, Grimmelshausen disregarded the big battles; more than Döblin, in fact, he took the limited perspective of the stupid but sly survivor, who could see no further than the winter quarters he happened to be in, the siege that had been dragging on for weeks, or the joys of foraging as the perspective of his narrative. Wallenstein isn't even mentioned in Grimmelshausen.

Bertolt Brecht later put this perspective on the stage in deliberate contrast to Schiller's *Wallenstein* trilogy, which concentrates throughout on "important events."

Tempting as it may seem to compare the testimonies and perspectives of German literature from Grimmelshausen to Döblin—and beyond, to Alexander Kluge's *Account of a Battle*—with regard to the Thirty Years' War and Operation Barbarossa,* I shall take no greater liberty than to commend Schiller's *History of the Thirty Years' War* to our attention; for clearly Döblin was a fact-intoxicated reader of that chronicle; he obviously exploited Schiller's industry; to him Schiller's historical treatise was material. No more? A few concordances are striking, such as Schiller's observation that Wallenstein had taken his belief that war must feed on war from Count Mansfeld—an insight, incidentally, that is acted out in Grimmelshausen and that in Brecht is raised to the level of a political principle; but Döblin spreads the image of self-nourishing war over every one of his pages. He shows us armies that descend on the country like plagues of locusts, devastate it, march on, and fight their battles as a kind of side line, between devastation and devastation.

Schiller's purpose was to make the Thirty Years' War intelligible as a clearly structured whole. One event follows from another. His ordering hand disclosed relationships, looked for meaning. More than once, Döblin deliberately smashes this whole construct to bits for the sake of reality. And their views of the Duke of Friedland himself [Wallenstein] are radically different.

*Code name for Hitler's invasion of the Soviet Union. —ED.

To simplify: Schiller's enlightened idealism puts the stress on the general and statesman in Wallenstein; Döblin shows us a banker tormented by gout. Time and again, he tells us that whenever Wallenstein is unable to avoid mounting a horse his stirrups are wrapped in wadding and silk. Wallenstein's army is the creation of a financial genius, and this is what distinguishes it from all other armies.

This is not the place to inquire to what extent Döblin's thesis is a historical correction of Schiller's *Wallenstein*; nor shall I measure Döblin's visionary picture by the findings of modern historiography, because, for one thing, I know of no historical work that so much as takes notice of Döblin, whether to refute, confirm, or correct him. Döblin's Wallenstein seems to be only incidentally a general. Now and then, when he cannot postpone or avoid a battle, he finds himself obliged to fight; but basically Döblin's Wallenstein is a modern manager, the first long-term military planner, the first architect of a powerful financial cartel that fed war and was fed by it, and has not been dismantled to this day. Wallenstein had the gift of promoting the most divergent interests and—as we shall see—combining them.

Four men—the Serbian Michna, the Dutch banker de Witte, the Jew Bassevi, leader of the Jewish business community in Prague, and the notorious Colonel von Wallenstein—exploit defeated Bohemia. Under the protection of Wallenstein's troops, the journeyman butcher Michna plunders the homes of the wealthy Bohemians. Paintings, jewels, gold, and silver are piled up in the Prague ghetto.

The Jews, those outcasts with the yellow caps and yellow stars, have learned between persecutions to appropriate and bury the wealth of their oppressors; they can't do much with it, just heap it up, look at it, and think of destroyed Jerusalem. This sorrowful pleasure is about all the Prague Jews have left, until Wallenstein gets there.

The banker de Witte suggests investing all this wealth and leasing the Bohemian mint. This suggestion, he owns, was made to him by two of his best clients: the respected Jewish businessman Bassevi, who has often helped the Emperor out financially, and a soldier who, despite certain acts of bravery in Venice and during the Battle of Prague, has a bad name in Bohemia: Colonel Albrecht von Wallenstein, the city commandant.

The Emperor needs money—the Emperor always needs money, and lots of it—so why not go into this promising business? A consortium is organized. For an annual rental of six million, the four businessmen take over the imperial mint in Prague. Soon it's only three who, with the help of the mint, regulate the circulation of money, for Wallenstein puts Michna the Serbian butcher under surveillance and soon under arrest, threatening to prosecute him for looting. Michna, he claims, hides his loot; he must hand over his silver, for the mint is short of raw material.

And then they mint to their heart's content. They clip the coinage, they adulterate it with base metal until only a suspicion of silver is left. Wallenstein's armed companies guard the mint day and night. They enlist paid and volunteer "buyers," who barge into the peasants' houses and gouge out their last ducats. Gangs are formed; imperial trumpeters proclaim on the streets and squares that all silver must be delivered to the mint. Whereupon all the silver disappears. Soon four new guilders are offered for one old reichstaler. Wallenstein, the biggest speculator in the land, is often seen standing by the coining punches, "a tall, hollow-chested man wearing a costly diamond necklace on his hat." He has a vision. His time will soon be at hand.

When the lease on the mint expired, the Emperor tried to go on minting. But he couldn't lay hands on anything that could be made into coins. Bassevi and de Witte had pulled out before the impoverished, infuriated people stormed the mint and found nothing but empty punches.

Wallenstein's fraudulent currency remained in circulation for only three months. The "long" guilder was reduced by decree to a sixth of its value. The government was declared bankrupt. The troops deserted. And Wallenstein, with his quickly swollen fortune, bought up new domains: Friedland and Reichenberg, Welisch, Schuwigara, and Gitschin.

All this, all his riches and lands, Wallenstein staked on one card. He offered his services to the Emperor, undertaking to raise a great imperial army to fight enemies at home and abroad, for then the Emperor would no longer be dependent on Maximilian of Bavaria and his army under Tilly, but could have a weapon against the onslaught of Christian, King of Denmark.

What do the diplomats in their whispered councils have to say about Wallenstein's magnanimity? "My friends, I've found out why Wallenstein is so strongly for the Emperor. He's advancing us the money for the army, but he expects the army to bring the money back to him from the empire with simple and compound interest. . . ."

The army as a capital investment. Döblin's retrospective vision is terrifying: long before Krupp made *his* big killing at Verdun, Wallenstein invested his fortune in armaments. Krupp and Wallenstein each bought himself an emperor. And we're still unwilling to recognize that Hitler didn't take over industry, but that the industrialists—Wallenstein's adepts—bought themselves their Hitler. In 1917 Army Doctor Döblin had good reason to look back from Verdun. Krupp and all those who demand a Krupp, like all those who make a Krupp possible, have their forerunners: a journeyman butcher, a banker, a Jewish businessman, and a colonel form a consortium and with it the material basis for the long life of a war that, interrupted by breathing spells that we call peace, is still going on. Schiller's heroes and their likes are at best gilt-edged securities in a portfolio, the rising prices of which can be imperiled only by the threat of peace negotiations. Since Döblin taught us to see Wallenstein as a master of high finance, we know that the reason for the failure of disarmament conferences is not always the lukewarmness of the conferees, but often enough the interests of an industry that has come to stand for the economic interests of all: disarmament might get us into difficulty. The Wallenstein system calls for standing armies.

This banker, the true victor of the Battle of the White Hill, made his entry into Vienna with twenty carriages. He was awaited with apprehension, with horror, but his money was wanted. Festivities, such as pageants and burnings of Jews, were organized for his edification. The word went around: "Here comes one of the latter-day alchemists, who turn Bohemian blood into gold." He stops at a merchant's house where one of his Prague partners, the Jewish businessman Bassevi, is already living. A crowd has formed outside. The chimney-sweeps are bellowing anti-Jewish songs. They call Wallenstein a prince of the Jews, because he is deliberately offending the pride of Vienna. His pact with the Jews, a motif that runs through all six parts of the work, merits our attention, because here Döblin confronts the causes of medieval anti-Semitism, which was Christian in character, with the here anticipated nineteenth-century emancipation of the Jews, while at the same time characterizing the beginnings of Zionism, its immense tenacity and ideological dangers.

Shortly before Wallenstein bargains for his monopoly, we see Bassevi the Jewish businessman conferring with five old men in a Prague synagogue. One of them is worried: If we gain glory and prestige by joining forces with Wallenstein, what happened to the Jews of Frankfurt will happen to the Jews of Prague; we'll be driven out of the city. To which the second man replied: They were only driven out for three years, after which the same trumpeter who drove them out blew them in again. Whereupon Bassevi observed that the Catholics had banished Calvinists and Lutherans from Bohemia, making room for the poor, hard-pressed Jews; so why not settle in Bohemia? The objection was: Even if they let us in, we won't go there, we won't settle. "What is written about the land of Bohemia? Where is anything written about the land of Bohemia? Nowhere. Should I leave my home like an old fool and settle in Bohemia?" To which his neighbor replied: "And how long do you and your children expect to sit here in the dark?"

The age-old answer, valid to this day, is: "Why ask? To us

Jews it's all as plain as day: If we're told to pack up our bundles and start for Jerusalem, praised be the Lord, I'll do it."

Bassevi attempted a compromise. Why not wait patiently for Jerusalem and meanwhile dwell in the light, side by side with the Christians? The counterargument: "If once the children of Israel start dwelling in the light, they will forget Jerusalem and be ashamed of being circumcised; they will barter Judaea for some worthless village in Bohemia."

The Jewish businessman and the five old men in the synagogue sighed. Bassevi found the solution: they would give the Emperor money and receive in return a trifling document authorizing the Bohemian Jews to engage in trade, henceforth and for all time, in the countryside, in the villages, and on the market places. And so it was concluded. But the Catholic Bohemians, who had just persecuted their fellow Christians with vicious dogs, fire, and torture and driven them out of the country, took this Jewish charter as an insult. Hatred burgeoned. At first Wallenstein was able to protect the Bohemian Jews; at first the banker Wallenstein needed the support of all those outcasts with the yellow caps and yellow stars. That was why he threw in his weight against the Viennese and calmly put up with being called the prince of the Jews.

In the days that follow, Vienna is showered with gifts of money. Wallenstein's dispatches descend on the Vienna chancelleries. Rudely, abruptly, he smacks the multidigit drafts of his banker de Witte down on the tables of dignitaries, father confessors, and ambassadors, who react to the magnitude of the gifts with an embarrassed, horrified laugh and pocket them.

What undermines the foundations of imperial Vienna is not the Turks or the armies of the Protestant Estates and Electors, but Wallenstein's money. For the Emperor grants Wallenstein an audience. The chamberlains are pleased, because he comes alone, without the Jew Bassevi. Döblin passes over the meeting between the Emperor and the usurer from Prague. A short wait in the antechamber; his cloak is removed; cut, as in a film. Wallenstein comes out, the Emperor is left alone. Bewildered, the Emperor puts his hand over his eyes. Who has been with him? It seems to him that he has seen that face, that he has "come across those soundlessly bright little eyes more than once."

The author condenses this first meeting between Wallenstein and Ferdinand into a dream vision of the Emperor. Dispensing with dialogue, negotiations, ruses, he fades into a closeup of the Emperor, resting buckled shoe on buckled shoe, groping for the arms of his chair, holding his hand over his eyes, until the vision takes over: he is riding over a mossy forest floor, as a soft breeze blows.

The colors grow lighter; the mouths of kittens have that light color, pale pink. It occurs to him that he has failed up until now to hear a gushing, a flowing of water. And then it's in the sky, over the earth, something black, wide, moving slowly. His horse is still running. He is unable to twist his body, to turn his face away from the breath that's blowing at him from above. . . . A hairy human chest is pressing down on him, hair is crawling over him like clouds or spider webs, human arms are held out, and he is riding toward them. But then a bulge—fleshy, smooth, slippery piglets, cold as the skin of a salamander. With elastic movements, swaying back and forth, it descends closer and closer to him. Caught up in ever more arms, he glides, he gasps for air, he pants. He's riding under the belly of a centipede. He has to bend lower on the restlessly rising and falling back of his horse. A soft surging of the belly takes his breath away; it's bloated, flopping sacks filled with air; for a few seconds he loses consciousness. His throat tries to expel an "ah, ah"; his ears fight for sound. And the tail of the monster strikes from above, uncoils from below like a whip, first striking the soles of his feet, sending a fierce electric shock to his heart, piercing his nostrils with fine needles, lethally penetrating deep, deep into his brain. Then it assails his navel from the front, whirls like a rotary drill into his stomach, his torso, his back. And now suddenly it resounds like an organ, roars immensely, meaninglessly from high to low, sustaining a shrill whistling note, gnashing by fits and starts like a dog tied by the paws to a stake, straining, stretching, stretching, straining, biting, biting.—He wakes up with a raucous scream, slowly removes his hand from his eyes, looks at his palm as if some of his dream had stuck to it, rubs it on his knee.

This dream, this condensation of all Wallenstein's fascination and menace, enhances the effect of the decrees and characters with which the Emperor favors the centipede and cartel builder. The calculation was simple and known to all concerned: "If Hapsburg doesn't raise an army, he will predictably be lost, along with the impotent Catholic League. If the League alone is victorious, the Emperor will be crushed in a few years by the Elector of Bavaria."

Accordingly, the Emperor promulgates a decree, naming the freshly appointed Duke of Friedland kapo over all the populations of the empire and the Netherlands. Bassevi and de Witte handle the financial end; this "Enabling Act" is put through in return for a loan of nine hundred thousand Rhenish guilders at 6 percent.

All the rest follows from this great financial transaction. Broadly conceived, confusing in its contradictions, yet quite logical as worked out in Wallenstein's mind. Quickly the regiments are mustered: "Take what you find." "If you can't hunt with a hawk, make do with a crow." Dangerous men, avid for spoils, troop to Wallenstein's colors; funds are extorted by the threat that troops will be quartered on the towns. Michna the journeyman butcher, who has been pardoned and re-ennobled in the meantime, requisitions grain for the expanding army, which floods the country and starts feeding on the war; at first a poorly armed raggle-taggle crowd, it quickly acquires equipment and becomes a perfect war machine. Wallenstein's calculations have worked out.

Here we shall not be able to study Döblin's fresco in detail. Though the book is titled *Wallenstein*, ample space is given to Maximilian and the League, to Gustavus Adolphus the puritan crusader, to the Saxon and Palatine, French and Bohemian intrigues of Count Slawata. And time and again to Ferdinand, who is said to trust Wallenstein as a woman trusts her husband.

An irresistibly fascinated Emperor, whose plan to humiliate Wallenstein—the holder of power, the personified will—developed along with his infatuation.

Döblin's epic sketch—for *Wallenstein* cannot be called a well-balanced, self-contained novel—ends with a scene that departs from all historical fact and ignores the vast accumulation of historical documents. Transported to the realm of fable, the Emperor flees. He withdraws from his court, from the empire, from secular power. At the end we see him foolish and babbling, removed from his responsibility and roaming about with marauders, now their anonymous equal. While the murder of Wallenstein is still presented in accordance with recognized categories, though it does not parallel Schiller's scenario—for it is not the traitor who dies but the creditor, to whom Emperor and empire are indebted—Ferdinand, the fugitive Emperor, is murdered by a goblinlike dwarf in the forest. The weapon is wielded with ecstatic joy. Of the Emperor nothing remains. The book, which was heavily burdened with documentary events and slowly advancing moraines of facts, culminates in dematerialized serenity and historyless unreality. Ferdinand seeks and finds silence. He dissolves into nothingness.

And yet this chapter, as visionary as the spark that released the whole complex (namely, the crossing of the Swedish fleet), reaches over into Alfred Döblin's next epic design. "Ferdinand's Death" is on the one hand the completion of *Wallenstein* and on the other the beginning of a futurist novel of adventure, *Mountains, Oceans, and Giants.* In his notes on this book, Döblin wrote: "When at the end of the war I brought *Wallenstein* home from Alsace-Lorraine without a final chapter, I groped about within myself to see how I could end it. The best way, I sometimes thought, would be not at all. Then, early in 1919, I was deeply moved by the sight of some black tree trunks on the street in Berlin. The Emperor Ferdinand must die, I thought."

It would be worthwhile to investigate to what extent and how frequently the image of tree trunks, with smooth, dry, or black, damp, sweating bark, among which something happens, may have influenced Döblin's work, or to what extent the author may have been aware of such a fixation. We remember: sitting in the casino park, the nearsighted army doctor sees the Swedish fleet sailing through the trees. We remember: Wallenstein meets the Emperor Ferdinand for the first time and sparks off a dream vision; the Emperor is riding among trees over a mossy forest floor; above him the hairy, breathing belly of a centipede. We hear: a wood goblin stabs the Emperor in the forest. "It was raining. The drops splattered as they fell. Ferdinand lay on two high branches. The cool water trickled over his bright eyes. The goblin had pulled little branches over himself; he sat covered by the foliage. Swinging his body on big branches, grumbling, frowning."

The seventh book of *Berlin Alexanderplatz* also ends in a forest. Again the forest is witness to a murder. Reinhold strangles Mieze. After the murder, a storm sets the forest in motion; nature joins in the action. But whereas *Wallenstein* brings the imperial recluse to an unidentified mythical forest, in *Berlin Alexanderplatz* the murder is committed in the Freienwald, near Berlin, a spot exactly localized as though a subsequent police report had been consulted.

Now I'm tempted to look for this forest motif, these wet, sweating tree trunks, in *Mountains, Oceans, and Giants*. The great scene after the Uralian War: Marduk, Prefect of the Mark, renounces scientific research, technology, progress. Himself a scientist, he arrests the scientific elite of the country and drives them into an experimental forest that he himself has cultivated. The forest begins to grow; the tree trunks expand, exude sticky sap, hem the scientists in, take their air, their breath, transform them into trees, which merge with one another, until in the end a shapeless mass of tropical vegetation absorbs the human spirit along with its quest for knowledge and destructive drive.

Between the Emperor's death in the mythical Bohemian forest and the murder of Biberkopf's Mieze in Freienwalde, near Berlin, Döblin conceived this futurist mass murder in a futurist forest, and to me, the reader, it seems that no book ever sprouted a forest more real than the synthetic product of Marduk the scientist, who wanted to put an end to all science, who, himself a destructive thinker, held thought to be the cause of all destruction, and encapsulated it in vegetation; only his idea remained outside and perpetuated itself.

But before I beguile you into futurist adventures, before I lose myself in *Mountains, Oceans, and Giants* and speak of tourmaline veils or the deglaciation of Greenland; before the luxuriant forests that spring up after the deglaciation set themselves in motion like animals and engulf Europe—

> . . . on the western edge of Hamburg, by the seaside, the advancing monsters devastated whole neighborhoods. The Senate's drastic security measures were futile, contributing only to the ruin of the megalopolis. The rays and burning projectiles ripped the beasts to pieces, but their parts, spewing liquid as they died, dragged themselves and other burgeoning creatures through the streets and parks. The most hideous shapes appeared. Charred trees, from the tops of which jutted long human hair, topped by human heads; hideous, gigantic faces of men and women. The tail fins of a sea monster, descending on a housing development at the edge of the city, gathered up quantities of inert objects, harrows, carts, plows, planks. This moving, sprouting, teeming mass absorbed potato fields, dogs, people. It rose like a cake, rose high, toppled over the fertile plain, rolled slowly, devastatingly forward like a mass of lava. And over the whole flowing, spreading mass grew trees, gigantic leaves. . . .

—before I let Marduk's experimental forest expand and devastate the city (and I haven't said a word about the jungles in the Amazonian novel, or about the judicial function of the forest in the Early Expressionist Buttercup story); before I follow this motif to the end of my biographical account (Döblin made his exit as an apple tree), I shall take refuge in the final phase of my homage to my teacher: anyone who becomes involved with him and his mythical, real, or visionary forests is ultimately in danger of getting lost in a jungle of wet, sweating, luxuriant trees, of losing the author amid books and theories that strive to cancel out and refute one another.

But that's what Döblin wanted: to hide behind his books. In response to an inquiry from a newspaper, he said in 1928: "As a doctor I am only remotely acquainted with the writer who bears my name." An autobiographical sketch tells us that he was born in 1878 in Stettin. And goes on: "Studied medicine, practiced for several years as an alienist, then went into internal medicine, is now a specialist, practicing in East Berlin."

Catchwords mark our search for the author. To what extent was his character imprinted by his father, a Stettin tailor who at the age of forty deserted his wife and five children and made off across the sea? Mulling over his own motivations, Döblin several times, with bitter irony, varied the story of his runaway father; but his own wanderlust, his longing to break away, worked itself out on maps and in archives. Prussian rigor chained him to East Berlin. Much as he was tempted to throw over the traces while on an excursion to Leipzig in April 1923, his sense of duty brought him back. "Ah," he sighed. "How lucky you people are in Leipzig. I must go back to Ziethen and Scharnhorst."*

In other words, a man who makes do with what he finds at hand. Siemens and Borsig give him his technology, their prospectuses give him the turbine myth. Shall we call him a sedentary demiurge? A modern Jean Paul surrounded by card files?

As I continue my search for the author, he remains small, nervous, jumpy, and nearsighted, but by no means indifferent to day-to-day politics or averse to direct action. Joined the USPD [Independent German Social Democratic Party] in 1921 and later the SPD [German Social Democratic Party]. His Prussian makeup enabled him, on the one hand, to participate patiently in the trivia of party politics and later, on the other hand, when the Social Democrats joined in voting for the "obscenity

---

*Hans Joachim von Ziethen (1699–1786), Prussian general under Frederick the Great. Gerhard Johann David von Scharnhorst (1755–1813), Prussian general, reorganized the Prussian army, fought against Napoleon. —ED.

law," to leave the party, but without feeling the need to proclaim that he had become more radical, experienced a great disillusionment, and burned all his bridges. Döblin was not afraid to live with his contradictions. "Distancing" oneself, that still-fashionable dance, was not his mode of locomotion. In countless articles he defended the cause of social democracy. Much as he admired Marx's "lucid historical and economic penetration of reality," he regarded twentieth-century Marxism as a doctrine of harsh centralism, economic determinism, and militarism. The health-insurance doctor of East Berlin declared that he belonged neither to the German nor to the Jewish nation; his nation, he said, comprised children and the insane.

Was he, then, a philanthropist and a visionary? A productive crank? An active Social Democrat who in his epic work *Manas* sings of a mystical India? Undoubtedly. And what else? A verbose disparager of art and a member of the Prussian Academy of Arts; an emancipated Jew and a Kierkegaardian Catholic; a sedentary Berliner and a footloose traveler on maps, until, with Hitler, the Kolbenheyers and Grimms took power,* until he was driven out of the country and banishment set him in motion against his will.

He returned home a French officer, bringing with him his latest novel, and couldn't find a publisher in the Federal Republic. His *Hamlet* was first published in 1956, and then in the German Democratic Republic. What is that turn of phrase so familiar in the land of poets and thinkers? "Forgotten in his lifetime." Döblin just wasn't right. He didn't go down. For the progressive left he was too Catholic; for the Catholics, too anarchistic; for the moralists he was short on rigid principles; for the late-night program, too awkward; for the educational radio, too vulgar. Neither *Wallenstein* nor *Giants* lent itself to consumption, and Döblin had the audacity to return in 1946 to a Ger-

*Erwin Guido Kolbenheyer (1878–1962), a mystically oriented nationalist writer hostile to Christian-Mediterranean civilization. Hans Grimm (1870–1959), author of *Nation Without Space*, known under the Nazi regime for his aggressively nationalistic writing. —ED.

many that was soon to dedicate itself to consuming. So much for the state of the market: Döblin's stock wasn't quoted and still isn't. One of his pupils and successors has inherited some of the fame that should have been his, and today I've tried to repay him in a small way.

In confining myself to the one futurist strain within Döblin's complex working system, which remained productive to the end; in calling attention to *Wallenstein* as evidence of a futuristic technique of the novel, setting aside the political, essay-writing, Catholic Döblin; in focusing, within the *Wallenstein* complex, on an analysis of the general as big banker, I can hope at the most, ten years after my teacher's death, to help arouse your curiosity, to tempt you, to help him find readers. He will upset you; he will trouble your dreams; he will make you gulp; you won't like the taste of him; you'll find him indigestible and he won't agree with you. He will change his reader. Anyone who is satisfied with himself should steer clear of Döblin.

THE TIN DRUM
IN RETROSPECT
or THE AUTHOR
AS DUBIOUS WITNESS

First published in Süddeutsche Zeitung, *January 12, 1974.*

In the spring and summer of 1952 I hitchhiked back and forth through France. I lived on nothing. I sketched on wrapping paper and, infected with logorrhea, wrote and wrote. Along with a number of (I believe) exceedingly derivative cantos about the pilot Palinurus, who fell asleep at the helm, I turned out an endlessly proliferating poem in which Oskar Matzerath, before taking on that name, made his appearance as a stylite saint.

A young man, an existentialist in accordance with the fashion of the day. A mason by trade. He lived in our times. A savage, rather haphazardly well read, he was not chary of quotations. Even before prosperity erupted, he was disgusted with prosperity and in love with his disgust. Right in the middle of his small town (which remained nameless) he therefore built himself a pillar and chained himself to the top of it. His vituperating mother handed up his meals in a dinner pail affixed to a pole. Her attempts to lure him down to earth were backed up by a chorus of young girls with mythological hairdos. The small-town traffic circled around his pillar, friends and enemies gathered, and in the end a whole community was looking up at him. He, the stylite, high above them all, looked down, nonchalantly alternating fixed leg and free-moving leg; he had found his perspective and reacted with a volley of metaphors.

This long poem was a flop; I left it somewhere and I remember only fragments, which show if anything how much I was influenced by Trakl, Apollinaire, Ringelnatz, Rilke, and the wretched German translations of Lorca, all at once. The only interesting feature was my quest for a perspective. But the stylite's elevated standpoint was too static. It took the diminutive three-year-old Oskar Matzerath to provide both distance and nobility. You might call Oskar Matzerath a converted stylite.

In the late summer of that same year, while crossing Switzerland on my way from southern France to Düsseldorf, I not only met Anna for the first time, but also saw something that took my saint down from his pillar. On an afternoon like any other, I saw a three-year-old boy with a tin drum among a group of coffee-drinking adults. What struck me and stayed with me was the three-year-old's self-forgetful concentration on his instrument, his disregard of the world around him (grownups chatting over their afternoon coffee).

For at least three years my "find" remained buried. I moved from Düsseldorf to Berlin, changed sculpture teachers, met Anna again, married her a year later, dragged my sister, who had got herself into a mess, out of a convent, sketched and modeled birdlike figures, grasshoppers, and filigree chickens, botched my first attempt at a prose piece, which was titled "The Barrier," was patterned on Kafka and derived its plethora of metaphors from the Early Expressionists. Only then did I succeed, being more relaxed, in writing my first occasional poems, casual offerings accompanied by drawings that took their distance from the author and acquired the independence that made them publishable: *The Advantages of Windhens* was the title, my first book.

With a baggage of stored-up material, vague plans, and precise ambition—I wanted to write my novel and Anna was looking for more rigorous ballet training—we left Berlin early in 1956, penniless but undaunted—and went to Paris. Not far from the Place Pigalle, Anna found an exacting Russian ballet teacher in the person of Madame Nora. And I, while still putting the finishing touches to my play *The Wicked Cooks*, set to work on the first draft of my novel, the title of which changed from *Oskar the Drummer* to *The Drummer* to *The Tin Drum*. At that precise point my memory cuts off. I remember that I drew up a number of outlines summing up my epic material and filled them with catchwords, but my outlines canceled one another out and were dropped as the work went on.

The manuscripts of the first, second, and finally third drafts fed the furnace that was located in my workroom, and of which I shall have more to say.

With the first sentence—"Granted: I am an inmate of a mental hospital . . ."—my block was gone, words pressed in on me, memory, imagination, playfulness, and obsession with detail gave themselves free rein, chapter engendered chapter. When a gap broke the flow of my story, I hopped over it; history came to my help with local offerings; little jars sprang open, releasing smells. I took on a wildly proliferating family; I argued with Oskar Matzerath and his clan about streetcar lines, about simultaneous events and the absurd pressure of chronology, about Oskar's right to tell his story in the first or the third person, about his desire to beget a child, about his real transgressions and his feigned feelings of guilt.

My attempt to give Oskar the loner a vicious little sister was thwarted by Oskar's objection; it seems quite possible that under the name of Tulla Pokriefke the impeded sister later insisted on her right to literary existence.

Far more distinctly than the process of writing I remember my workroom: a damp hole on the ground floor. It was also my studio, but once I started putting *The Tin Drum* on paper, my attempts at sculpture crumbled away. My workroom was also the furnace room for the tiny two-room apartment upstairs. My activities as stoker and writer were closely meshed. Whenever the writing process met with a snag, I'd go and get two buckets of coke out of the cellar. My workroom smelled of mold and, cozily, of gas. Dripping walls kept my imagination flowing. The dampness of the room may have encouraged Oskar Matzerath's wit.

Once a year, during the summer months, I was allowed, because Anna is Swiss, to write for a few weeks in the fresh air of the Ticino. I sat at a stone table in a grape arbor, gazed at the shimmering subtropical stage set, and, sweating, wrote about the frozen Baltic.

Sometimes, for a change of air, I'd scribble outlines of chapters in the kind of Paris bistros one sees in old movies: surrounded by tragically enlaced lovers, old women hidden in their coats, wall mirrors, and Art Nouveau decorations, I'd write something about elective affinities: Goethe and Rasputin.

And yet during all that time I must have lived strenuously, cooked helpfully, and, out of the pleasure I took in Anna's dancing legs, danced whenever opportunity offered. Because in September 1957—I was in the midst of the second draft—our twin sons, Franz and Raoul, were born. The problem wasn't literary, only financial. We lived on the carefully apportioned three hundred marks a month that I earned more or less in passing. Sometimes I think the mere fact of not graduating from secondary school, much as it distressed my father and mother, saved me. With a degree I'd have become a night-program director and kept my manuscript in a drawer, and because I was prevented from writing I'd have piled up an increasing grudge against all those free-ranging scribblers whom their heavenly father feedeth all the same.

My work on the final draft of the chapter about the defense of the Polish Post Office in Danzig necessitated a trip to Poland in the spring of 1958. Höllerer arranged it; Andrzej Wirth wrote out an invitation, and I went to Gdansk via Warsaw. On the assumption that some of the defenders of the Polish Post Office would still be alive, I inquired at the Polish Ministry of the Interior, which maintained a bureau devoted to the documentation of German war crimes in Poland. There I was given the addresses of three former Polish postal clerks (most recent address dating from 1949), but informed that these alleged survivors had not been recognized by the Polish Postal Workers Union (or any other official body), because in the fall of 1939 it had been reported by both German and Polish official sources that these men had all been court-martialed and shot; that their names had accordingly been incised in a memorial tablet, and that people incised in stone are dead.

In Gdansk I looked for Danzig, and found two of the former Polish postal clerks. In the meantime, they'd gone to work in the shipyard, where they earned more than they had at the post office. They were for the most part satisfied with their unrecognized status. But their sons wanted to see their fathers as heroes and tried (without success) to get them recognized as resistance fighters. From the two post-office employees (one had delivered money orders) I obtained detailed accounts of what happened in the post office during its defense. Their escape routes are something I could not have made up.

In Gdansk I retraced the itineraries of a Danzig schoolboy, spoke in graveyards with tombstones that made me nostalgic, sat (as I had sat as a boy) in the reading room of the municipal library, leafing through piles of the *Danziger Vorposten.* I smelled the Mottlau and the Radaune. In Gdansk I was a stranger, but in fragments I rediscovered everything: bathing establishments, walks in the woods, brick Gothic, and the apartment house on Labesweg between Max-Halbe-Platz and Neuer Markt; and revisited (on Oskar's advice) the Church of the Sacred Heart: the same old Catholic fug.

Then I stood in the kitchen–living-room of my Kashubian great-aunt Anna. She didn't believe me until I showed her my passport: "My goodness, Günter child, you've gotten so big." I stayed awhile and listened. When the defenders of the Polish Post Office surrendered, her son Franz had indeed been shot. I found his name incised in stone on the memorial tablet: officially recognized.

In the spring of 1959, when I'd finished work on my manuscript, corrected the galleys, and dispatched the page proofs, I was given a four-month travel grant. Once again Höllerer had pulled strings. The idea was for me to go to the United States and answer students' questions about now and then. I never went. To get a visa in those days you had to submit to an exacting medical examination. I submitted and was told that tuberculomas—bonelike nodules—had been found here and there in my lungs; when tuberculomas break open, cavities form.

For that reason—and also because by that time de Gaulle had come to power in France and after one night in the custody of the Paris police I was overcome by a positive longing for the West German police—we left Paris soon after *The Tin Drum* was published (and left me), and moved back to Berlin. There I had to take afternoon naps, do without liquor, get examined at regular intervals, drink cream, and three times daily ingurgitate little white pills that, I believe, were called Neoteben—all of which cured me and made me fat.

But while still in Paris I had done some preparatory work on the novel *Dog Years*, which was originally called "Potato Peelings" and got off to a bad start. It took my novella *Cat and Mouse* to make me drop this short-winded project. But by then I was already famous and didn't have to stoke the furnace any more while writing. Since then I've found it harder to write.

KAFKA AND
HIS EXECUTORS

First published in L 76, *no. 9 (1978).*

"Judge for yourself," said Olga, "I warn you it sounds quite simple, one can't comprehend at first why it should be of any importance. There's a great official in the Castle called Sortini." "I've heard of him already," said K., "he had something to do with bringing me here." "I don't think so," said Olga, "Sortini hardly ever comes into the open. Aren't you mistaking him for Sordini, spelt with a 'd'?" "You're quite right," said K. "Sordini it was." "Yes," said Olga. "Sordini is well known, one of the most industrious of officials, he's often mentioned; Sortini on the other hand is very retiring and quite unknown to most people. More than three years ago I saw him for the first and last time. It was on the third of July at a celebration given by the Fire Brigade, the Castle too had contributed to it and provided a new fire engine. Sortini, who was supposed to have had some hand in directing the affairs of the Fire Brigade, but perhaps he was only deputizing for someone else—the officials mostly hide behind each other like that, and so it's difficult to discover what any official is actually responsible for—Sortini took part in the ceremony of handing over the fire engine. There were of course many other people from the Castle, officials and attendants, and true to his character Sortini kept well in the background."*

I have chosen to preface my remarks on the tenth anniversary of the occupation of Czechoslovakia with this passage from

*Franz Kafka, *The Castle*, trans. Willa and Edwin Muir (London and New York: Alfred A. Knopf, 1930). —Ed.

Franz Kafka's unfinished novel *The Castle,* begun in 1922, because of the insight it provides into the "Kafkaesque" nature of bureaucracy. Since there are plenty of political analyses of the events leading up to August 21, 1968, I shall try to derive from Kafka's vision of totalitarian administration a few questions about the structures to which, quite apart from military, economic, and ideological power, the societies of East and West are more subject than ever.

How is the activity of Sortini and Sordini being continued? Who, or what compelling force, blurs the dividing lines between jurisdictions? Why is it that one and the same man can be responsible for everything and for nothing? In what relation to each other do bureaucracy and corruption increase and decrease? When do administrative apparatuses become supernatural and symbolic in Kafka's sense?

There are no simple answers to these questions, because bureaucracy, even in the vulgar realm of the anteroom, is ambivalent by nature; the closer one gets to the Castle, the more one loses sight of its outlines. In a bureaucracy, regardless of the ideology it serves, power is subdivided into many-layered and seemingly crisscrossing administrative channels. No longer in the old-fashioned Austro-Hungarian style known to Kafka, but geared to the present and future, equipped with modern technology, yet unchanging in its anonymity, or at the most wavering between Sortini and Sordini, this bureaucratic system holds men and women in its clutches, classifies them, purports to protect them, is omnipresent, and keeps the individual—official and private citizen alike—under control in the name of laws old and new or entangles him in illegalities.

All ideological powers that advance a worldwide claim to exclusive possession of the truth, and therefore exclude one another and often fight one another to the death, are subject to one international order: bureaucracy. It considers itself omnipotent. It backs itself up. The ideological system may change, but the bureaucracy continues to function almost without a hitch, because, free as it is from value judgments, it has no difficulty in integrating itself with any new system. Nothing can take its place. Even in the midst of political turmoil, of revolutionary chaos, it will trust to its own law and endure; not even its smell will change.

Such stamina is convincing. When so much is going down the drain, permanence is what's wanted. What would we know about ourselves and one another if registration forms, questionnaires, identification papers, personal files, etc., didn't live after us—a timeless filing system. Nothing would come to light if not for those paper deposits of human existence known as documents.

For instance: without the all-preserving bureaucracy it would not have been possible to obtain an only-too-clear picture of the navy judge and future Prime Minister of Baden-Württemberg Hans Filbinger.* It's almost frightening to think that we owe so much knowledge to the bureaucracy. The fact that Filbinger, who himself collected data about others, fell a victim to this very method does not make the method any less questionable; it merely shows that partisan forbearance, not to say mercy, is alien to bureaucracy. Rank and name mean nothing to its memory. If Filbinger were called Fildinger and the two were confounded like Kafka's Sortini and Sordini, the bureaucrats in Kafka's Castle, Fildinger, who never became prime minister but remained a successful jurist, would have nothing to fear even if the knowledge concerning him, obtainable with the help of the bureaucracy, were even more horrifying than the knowledge that horrified us in connection with Filbinger. The case assumed importance only because he was Prime Minister.

Because if not for his high office and if not for democratic sensibilities concerning high-ranking officials, Filbinger as well as Fildinger would have managed the transition from the Na-

*In 1978 Filbinger was forced to resign his premiership after twelve years, in the wake of revelations concerning a death sentence he had pronounced as a naval judge in the last days of the Hitler regime. —Ed.

tional Socialist power structure of the Greater German Reich to the German Federal Republic just about perfectly: always faithful to the law, he went right on collecting data about others. Even if Filbinger isn't allowed to do it any more, Fildinger is as industrious as ever.

In this sense Sortini and Sordini have also remained faithful to each other: coordinated with changing intelligence services, they are still doing their duty. They are interchangeable. They can be identified only with those paper activities, at all times protected by law, that have come to seem timeless and that constitute the essence of bureaucracy, never with ideological labels that can be invoked and repudiated.

Despite serious attempts at democratic reform, the administrative machine suffered no substantial damage after the collapse of the fascist power structure; it is still so efficient that, if properly fed—with the so-called Antiradical Decree, for example—it can sweep aside all reformist barriers and operate once again without value judgments—in other words, as a law unto itself. And, similarly, the substance of the bureaucratic apparatus has been preserved in the country that provided the writer Franz Kafka with palpable realities. Despite confusing ideological vicissitudes, the Castle of Kafka's novel has managed, from the long-past days of the Austro-Hungarian Empire down to the communist present, to preserve its rich metaphorical significance; it has turned away and worn down thousands of surveyors and seekers after the truth. It has even grown in all directions. Higher, wider, with more ample basements, the Castle now rests also on an ideological foundation.

Now that the party bureaucracy of Leninist-Stalinist communism has infiltrated the "normal," home-grown bureaucracy, bending all its organs to one supreme will, the individual is totally at the mercy of its anonymous power.

In Kafka's novel *The Trial*, the accused Josef K. never finds out what he is accused of or who has condemned him. True, the surveyor K., partly through obstinacy and partly with the help of women he cleverly makes use of, gains some acquaintance with castellans and middle-level officials, but he never gets into the Castle, never penetrates the inner structure of the power that holds him in its grip. He gets mixed up in plots and sub-plots. Sometimes he seems to have forgotten the reason behind his efforts. He involves himself in guilt. He runs himself ragged. The ways of the bureaucracy wear him out.

The story of this calvary was written decades ago and has become a modern classic. And the blueprint of the future that the author has left us in the form of a vision as precise as it is rich in implications, has been overtaken and given reality in all totalitarian countries, where power structure and administration have become identical. Not least in the land of its origin. The Socialist People's Republic of Czechoslovakia preserved its bureaucratic machine virtually unimpaired through the Prague Spring, that desperate attempt at reform. True, the occupation of Czechoslovakia in 1968 marks a date in the history of power politics, but the tanks of the occupying powers were set in motion long before that. By the early sixties both sides were flexing their muscles. This mustering of forces is reflected in a peripheral occurrence that perhaps, more than any high-level political action, throws light on the causes of the lasting conflict. Among other things, there was talk at the time of the surveyor K.

On May 27 and 28, 1963, a group of philosophers, writers, and literary scholars met in Liblice Castle in Bohemia to discuss the work of an author whose books had hitherto been regarded as suspect if not taboo, and whose collected works have yet to be published in any Eastern-bloc country.

If we bear in mind that the idea of peaceful coexistence had gained ground since the Twentieth Party Congress of the Soviet Union, and moreover that criticizing Stalinism had become permissible within certain limits, the Kafka Conference at Liblice Castle can be seen as an early harbinger of the Prague Spring.

All those who attended regarded themselves as Marxists.

More or less directly, often with passion, though sometimes rather timidly and with reservations, a total of twenty-seven speakers, all professing the Marxist faith, certified that Franz Kafka, despite his pessimistic view of life, was nevertheless a humanist writer and therefore a part of the communist-humanist heritage. He was termed "progressive."

Ridiculous as these assessments look now, they were necessary at the time—a gesture perhaps, but without such a gesture it would not have been possible to talk about Kafka. Whether put forward with conviction or with tongue in cheek, the certification of the hitherto banned or ignored author as a humanist opened the way for further discussion.

"The Conference," it was later reported, "addressed itself to the ideological clarification of the literary problems connected with Kafka's work. Some speakers, of course, raised questions of cultural policy and first of all the question of whether Kafka's works should be published. Here again an exchange of opinions was helpful, though of course the Conference neither was nor could be empowered to take a hand in solving these questions."

The subsequent fate of some Conference participants shows what upheavals communism has since undergone. The chairman of the Conference, Eduard Goldstücker, was president of the Czechoslovakian Writers' Union during the short-lived Dubček era; today he is a refugee, living in England. The Austrian communist Ernst Fischer was expelled from the Austrian party for protesting against the occupation of Czechoslovakia. By decision of the Central Committee, Roger Garaudy was expelled from the French Communist Party.

At the end of his address, Garaudy quoted a conversation between Kafka and his friend Gustav Janouch about Picasso. On the occasion of the first Cubist exhibition in Prague, Janouch said, "That is arbitrary deformation." Kafka replied, "I don't think so. He merely takes note of the distortions that have not yet penetrated our consciousness: Art is a mirror. Like a clock, it is—sometimes—ahead of time."

The comparison between Picasso and Kafka was not taken

up by other speakers. No one else was prepared to go so far. But some tried to show that Kafka had been drawn to socialism as a young man. Many insisted that Kafka, more than anyone else, had disclosed the alienation of man under capitalism. The Western bourgeois critics were attacked for surrounding Kafka with mystery and suppressing his social criticism.

To this the Polish philosopher Roman Karst replied: ". . . bourgeois criticism has been accused of misinterpreting Kafka's work; it has even been claimed that Kafka needs to be defended against bourgeois criticism. To take this position is to forget that in all the years since the Second World War we haven't written a word about Kafka. . . . We've been warned that Kafka must be read sensibly. But can a poet be read sensibly? In my opinion he should be read and above all published."

Ernst Fischer called on the assembly to put Kafka to socialist use:

Kafka is a writer who concerns us all. The alienation of man, which he exposed with maximal intensity, attains frightening proportions in the capitalist world. But it has certainly not been overcome in the socialist world. To overcome it step by step in the fight against dogmatism and bureaucracy, for socialist democracy, initiative, and responsibility, is a long-drawn-out process and a major task. The reading of such works as *The Trial* and *The Castle* is likely to help us accomplish this task. In these works the socialist reader will find aspects of his own problems, and the socialist functionary will be obliged to consider certain questions more thoroughly and with more attention to distinctions and shadings.

The Prague journalist and translator Alexei Kusák went a step further:

The fact that Kafka has written about absurdities that might just as well be ours, that Kafkaesque situations provide the model for situations known to us in socialist countries from the days of the personality cult, speaks for Kafka, for his brilliance at creating types, for his artistic method. Thanks to this method, he recognized that increasingly impenetrable social relations combined with unchallengeable institutional power give rise, day after day, to absurd situations in which innocent persons are accused of crimes they did not commit. . . .

Other speakers went so far as to draw a comparison between the always active, urgently seeking, and occasionally violent surveyor K. of *The Castle* and the passive, evasive fugitive Josef K. of *The Trial*, and to make the surveyor something of a pioneer and revolutionary. Goldstücker drew a parallel between the surveying and the distribution of land. This attempt to claim Kafka not only as a humanist but also as a revolutionary for communist home use was rightly contested: Franz Kafka cannot be identified with any ideology; he foresaw the future of all the ideological movements of his day.

In his biography of Kafka, Heinz Politzer quotes a passage from Gustav Janouch's *Conversations with Kafka*, relating to an incident that took place in 1920. The two friends met a group of workers bound for a meeting carrying flags and banners. Kafka said: "These people are so self-possessed, so self-confident and good-humored. They rule the streets and that makes them think they rule the world. They are mistaken. Behind them stand the secretaries, officials, and professional politicians, all the modern sultans for whom they are preparing the way to power." And when Janouch asked Kafka if he thought the Russian Revolution would spread, he replied: "As a flood spreads, the water becomes shallower and dirtier. The Revolution evaporates, leaving behind it only the muck of a new bureaucracy. The chains of tormented mankind are made of red tape."[*]

A man who speaks like this cannot derive a progress-myth from the irresistible historical process; he suffers history. Kafka's view of the world was apocalyptic. This too was discussed and debated at the Conference. After the supposed end

---

[*]Gustav Janouch, *Conversations with Kafka*, trans. Goronwy Rees (New York: New Directions, 1968, pp. 119–120). (Translation slightly modified.) —Ed.

of Stalinism, the conferees were intent on preparing the way for a new historical phase; and they held that, whichever way one looked at it, there should be a place for Kafka in the "communism with a human face" which the Czechoslovakian reformers, the architects of the Prague Spring, were then trying to build.

It has become a commonplace to characterize the world of administrative red tape, the reduction of human existence to documentary records, and the relationship between bureaucracy and corruption as Kafkaesque. Kafka's meticulous description of the official hierarchy, the imaged contrast he repeatedly draws between bureaucratic zeal and an inefficiency that merely stirs up dust, this paper world that Kafka built up from words and set before the reader in *The Castle* makes it possible to draw comparisons with the extra-literary world. Yet to see Kafka's surveyor K. exclusively as a fighter against the twofold evil of bureaucracy and corruption is to belittle Kafka's work. The surveyor can be interpreted every bit as plausibly as a seeker after God and truth. The impenetrable, unattainable Castle can be taken as a metaphor for the theological concept of grace. And although *The Trial* describes the mills of earthly justice in terrifying detail, a reader can equally well identify it with a supreme heavenly authority. Faustian traits have been attributed to the surveyor K. And Kafka's labyrinthine work can also be associated, quite convincingly, with the concepts of Jewish mysticism. Actually, the abundance of possible interpretations, including the most excessive, merely shows that works of literature—as of art in general—have and must have many meanings, because they are subservient not to the rites of logic but to the laws of aesthetics.

The demand for a single correct and universally valid interpretation usually springs from ideological or moral requirements. Wherever there is only a single reality, a single true doctrine and ethic, a desperate need arises for a single valid interpretation of artistic works. (There you see art as a milkable cow. And bitter as it may taste, what is milked from the cow must correspond to the universal conception of milk.)

Accordingly, my attempt to interpret Franz Kafka's writings, and especially his novel *The Castle*, as a commentary on totalitarian bureaucracy can apply only to one aspect of his work. But the relevance of this aspect is shown not only by the novel's rich detail, but also by the reality of the present period, which each day earns the epithet "Kafkaesque" anew.

And since the bureaucracies of Eastern as well as Western obedience are coming to resemble one another more and more, they raise their totalitarian claim that man is a being who is fully comprehensible on the basis of government files, with such omnipotence (as though beyond all earthly control) that they take on a diffuse, almost transcendent dimension, which can be termed divine or, if you will, Kafkaesque.

I am convinced that, at the time of its writing, Kafka's Castle metaphor, in both its earthly-bureaucratic and its theological sense, was visionary in character; today it has become extra-literary reality. Reality has outrun Kafka's vision of the future. In Prague and West Germany Kafka has found his executors.

Throughout the world we see the proliferation of bureaucratic structures that in their high-handedness not only evade the democratic control that has been attempted here and there, but also defy any rational explanation. The bureaucracy of our day is godlike in its absurdity. Though devised and operated by human beings, it becomes a law unto itself, transcends man, and only then, as it approaches perfection, begins to reveal the superhuman design that must have been present in Kafka's mind.

It would seem that the bureaucracy of our day is no longer earthly enough to be abolished by administrative reforms or even by a revolutionary clean sweep. Such attempts have occurred. Government by and for the people. More democracy! These have been the slogans. Thousands have assembled in protest, prepared to "march through the offices and institutions." Where are these people now? In what chancelleries have they become as interchangeable as Sortini and Sordini?

At the latest since the bureaucracy has been outfitted with the most recent technical improvements, we have been aware of the dangers inherent in all-powerful apparatuses identified with the materialized concept of God. We are no longer dealing with bureaucratic abuses, which can after all be remedied, but with a "legitimately" imposed fate. And so—in Prague or here at home—we resign ourselves. And so—in Prague and here at home—we have the audacity to protest. Like the surveyor K. we try to decode the hierarchy of the Castle administration, find out what's going on in the Castle by means of bribery if need be.

The Castle takes pity on us. For just as the so-called assistants Jeremias and Arthur are assigned to the surveyor K., so we too are favored with spies, in the form either of "bugs" or of the classic two-man team. They are helpful to us. They are our guardian angels. They see to it that we make no mistakes —in the higher sense. They anticipate our actions. They are programmed with more data concerning ourselves than we, with our pathetic earthly memories, could retain. They are one of the proofs of divine favor that the all-embracing bureaucracy offers us in both the down-to-earth and the transcendent sense.

And because Kafka's castellans and under-castellans, like our lower, middle, and high officials, groan under the burden and responsibility of their bureaucratic duty, as does the afflicted citizen under the supervision and burdensome favor of the bureaucracy, and even more, because reform-minded officials, on their own initiative or at the behest of the administered citizenry, are trying valiantly to accelerate the circulation of documents, to build up a counterbureaucracy by making the administration accountable, to humanize administrative offices with the help of potted plants, to give the snooping apparatus democratic visibility, and to protect our personal data, once stored, from ourselves and others, it seems safe to say that we all, the surveyor K. and the castellans, our middle- and upper-level officials, all those affected by the bureaucracy, are workers in the Lord's vineyard.

For that is how the bureaucracy, in Prague and at home in the Federal Republic, would like us to see it. Even if we cannot gain an overall view of the whole, whatever the whole may be —Castle or vineyard or the state with its absolute claim—we are a part of that whole and are thought indispensable as long as we remain active in the Lord's vineyard. We should till the soil, and it's all right if we groan. We must be conscious of our relative limitations—not everyone can know, let alone do, everything. Even from lofty positions, the whole can't always be comprehended. And so it comes about that certain highly placed, supposedly powerful gentlemen, who might be thought to have everything under control, have lately been making gestures of helplessness.

Not long ago, for instance, Chairman Erich Honecker was heard entreating the East German bureaucracy for Marx-Engels's sake—and for the sake of their socialist fellow men—to be less bureaucratic. Of course his plea remained unanswered, for despite its multiformity the bureaucracy has no mouth.

And back home in West Germany the chancellor and his ministers complain eloquently of a remotely similar helplessness. What grieves them is that when the legislation proposed by the chancellor and his ministers has been fed into the bureaucratic machine and returned to them after the requisite period of digestion, they can't recognize it. True, the machines operate smoothly, more so in fact than ever before, but they no longer comply with their instructions.

Here, for instance, is how one observer summarized the situation: The Antiradical Decree has long been virtually null and void, but this the bureaucracy refuses to recognize. On the contrary, it is more determined than ever to draw the most extreme consequences from this decree, which was issued many years ago but has meanwhile been several times attenuated, and has at last been virtually suspended. The bureaucracy has evidently declared its independence. Though fully recognizing the efficiency of our civil service, we must acknowledge this unfortunate fact.

So the guilty party has been found—or would be if he'd let you speak to him. The powerful clear themselves by putting the blame on the bureaucracy. It turns progressive laws into their reactionary opposite. It is a state within the state.—Wouldn't it be sensible and helpful to our constitutional state to smuggle as many radicals as possible into the civil service so as to disrupt the state within the state?

Ten years ago in Prague and at home in West Germany, many of us were resolved to storm the bureaucratic Castles and defeat the state within the state. Let's not forget that the Prague Spring had a short-lived West German counterpart in the student protest movement. Everywhere, in Paris, Warsaw, Berlin, and Prague, the slogan went out: "All power to the imagination." But only in Prague did the movement go beyond protest.

A few years after the Kafka Conference in Liblice Castle, the first sign of a far-reaching development, the Prague Spring, began to take on political importance. It was then that I made my first trip to Czechoslovakia, which was followed by many visits up to the year after the occupation. This also marks the beginning of my correspondence with the Czech writer Pavel Kohout, which, under the heading "Letters Across the Border," was published first in the German weekly *Die Zeit* and then in the Prague magazine *Student*.

The mere fact that, against a political background—in Czechoslovakia the neo-Stalinist Novotny era, and in West Germany a Social Democratic Party hamstrung by its involvement with the Great Coalition—a Communist and a Social-Democratic writer took what should be the self-evident step of carrying on a critical and self-critical discussion in correspondence form was unusual, a break with the dismal historical truism that Communists and Socialists were mortal enemies. Skeptical as Kohout and I were about our own and, it goes without saying, each other's political opinions, our letters were not devoid of hope. Kohout thought Communism was capable of reform; I was confident that the Social Democrats would change radically and effect a synthesis between democracy and socialism. We both thought this synthesis had a future.

And when Novotny was forced to resign and a new era began with Alexander Dubček, it looked as if in Czechoslovakia, the only Communist country with a democratic tradition, the mountain might move and our hopes become reality. For a few months the daily life of Czechoslovakia showed that democracy and socialism are essential to each other. The yoke of the omnipresent party bureaucracy seemed to have been thrown off. Because everyone spoke openly and because everyone experimented with his free speech as with an unaccustomed luxury and let it sparkle in public, people thought they had shaken off the customary snoopers and thrown them out of work. Proud, though still astonished and somewhat incredulous, people proved to one another that freedom of speech and Communism are not necessarily incompatible. They were even beginning to think the Communist brother countries had realized how useful such a reform could be to them when the armored Communism of the Soviet Union put an end to this great, theoretically sound, but spontaneous experiment.

Or, to put it more accurately, within the sphere of Soviet power the attempt to breach the Leninist-Stalinist structure of dogmatic Communism—in other words, the dictatorship of the party bureaucracy—was crushed. In the West, however, the impulsion given by Prague is still at work. Without it the Communist parties of Western Europe would not have developed so palpably, would not have developed so differently from one another or become so free of Soviet influence. It took the manifestation and failure of democratic socialism in Czechoslovakia to make the Socialist and Social-Democratic parties of Western Europe aware once more of their own aims: to give them a yardstick. Only the "New Left"—a vestige of the student protest movement—remained a prisoner to theory and broke up into splinter groups and sects; the lesson of Prague had taught these people nothing.

Nevertheless, I believe that any analysis of the events of 1968 must prove inadequate if it seeks their causes exclusively in military, economic, and ideological factors. My belief that Kafka had found his executors is based on the increased power of the bureaucracy. In its characteristic anonymity it survived the political change from Novotny to Dubček and from Dubček to Husak. In no time it was functioning again. In all likelihood it went right on working during the democratic interlude. At the most it may, confident in its indispensability, have relaxed temporarily, a possibility that is always open to it. It is self-perpetuating, timeless. Man's permanent need for security feeds its organs. Every new law—however well-meaningly it may purport to simplify the existing security arrangements —engenders new administrative departments, which, after the new departments are combined with older ones, proliferate in ever new subdivisions, and daily demonstrate their utility.

The social security which is indispensable to man and which in many instances has won legal status through years of political struggle, requires organization, requires a regularity unaffected by political value judgments. It is this regularity that assures the individual as well as society of pensions, education, disability, accident and unemployment insurance—that, in other words, insures him against a multiplicity of perils, and even promises to protect him against the enemies of state and society.

And so, we need the bureaucracy. If we could and wished to abolish it, we would be left uninsured in the midst of chaos. For many years Kafka was in the employ of the Workers' Accident Insurance Company. Burdensome as he found the work, he knew how useful it was in view of the frequency of work accidents and the inadequacy of accident insurance. If necessary, one source of energy—oil, coal, water power—could be substituted for another; but if the bureaucracy were destroyed, it could only be replaced by a modernized, more comprehensive bureaucracy.

That is what is happening. Stuffy offices and bulky filing cabinets are on the way out. The bureaucracy has occasionally been defended on the ground that it creates and preserves jobs; that argument will not be valid for long, because, in line with the general rationalization process affecting even the job-intensive bureaucracy, computers large and small, data banks, steadily improved electronic equipment, multimedia information centers, and other products of the second technological revolution will soon have replaced—or, in euphemistic parlance, "liberated"—Kafka's castellans, under-castellans, and their successors, the clerks and office managers.

We call this "progress" and it rather frightens us. True, these progressive developments will—and the process has already begun—do away with our traditional concepts of work as self-fulfillment or as servitude; the blue- and white-collar workers thus liberated will feel just as alienated in their excessive leisure time as they did before in their accustomed jobs. Worse: this predictable but unprepared-for change will not change the nature of the bureaucracy. At best the bureaucracy will be perfected. It will proliferate, because so much inactivity demands innumerable "leisure bureaus" to administer it, safeguard it, and protect it against misuse. Inactive masses tend to get out of control. They form crowds and are capable of irrational emotions. Supposedly grown aimless, the inactive masses might seek an aim outside the legal order. While the surveyor K. stormed the Castle in vain, masses of K.'s might be destructively successful and smash the mechanisms that have set them free.

But the new bureaucracy will also insure itself against these programmed dangers, either by feeding the leisure society with short-lived aims and even allowing limited revolutionary amusements, or by further developing the modern police state along Orwellian lines. Of course the West will accomplish this development more quickly, but quite possibly the ideologically monolithic East will go the same way, though with the usual time lag. What else can the rest of the world—whether East- or West-oriented—do but learn and emulate, especially since in the still traditionally structured countries of Asia, Africa, and South America the masses find themselves abandoned to unemployment and will therefore feel the need to catch up with the more advanced countries by developing a total bureaucracy capable of administering, protecting, and controlling them.

This future dimension is already discernible. It is common to all ideologies. The question of an alternative can only be answered radically—that is, by getting at the root. Anyone wishing to reject the bureaucracy with its system of safeguards must choose risk in the place of security. Anyone who chooses risk must either go to the dogs with terrorism or take up a long, hard struggle. Anyone who chooses risk must try, like Franz Kafka's surveyor K., to reach the perpetually receding Castle.

Today it is the signatories of Charter 77* who like Kafka's surveyor K. have chosen risk and rejected the offer of total security. Regardless of whether Kafka's novel *The Castle* is interpreted as a faithful picture of total bureaucracy or as a metaphor for the quest for ultimate truth, all the people I have been talking about are on their way to the Castle. We don't know if they'll get there. Their risk leaves the question open. And Kafka's novel remains a fragment.

I haven't set out to write one more analysis of the familiar power structure, or a political and ideological evaluation of

---

*In 1977 a manifesto known as Charta 77 was signed by more than seven hundred Czechoslovakian intellectuals, appealing to their government for greater freedom. —Ed.

Czechoslovakian reformed Communism and its failure, but, rather, in the light of August 21, 1968, to concentrate on the conference at Liblice Castle, which, though peripheral, definitely pointed the way to the Prague Spring. In conclusion, therefore, I shall go back to literature and its effects.

Not only has the writer Franz Kafka been interpreted *ad infinitum*; he has also produced epigones. We must not let these epigones—some justified in their ambiguity, others merely fashionable—blind us to the fact that a few writers managed to follow Kafka while preserving their independence.

Last year *Approximation,** a book of short stories by my colleague Hans Joachim Schädlich, appeared in the German Federal Republic. Schädlich had been unable to find a publisher for it in the German Democratic Republic. He has emigrated to West Germany with his family. Even more than the title story, the short tale "Under the Eighteen Towers of the Tyn Church" shows how a modified form of Kafka's Castle is still with us today and how, with the help of modern technology, bureaucracy in the guise of a State Security Service safeguards and totally controls the helpless citizen. The story, which with slight variations could take place in the Federal Republic, is set in the Prague of 1968 and in East Berlin. Two young citizens of the German Democratic Republic happen to be in Prague when the tanks arrive. A Western television reporter meets them in a doorway and they answer his questions. The East German police view the television footage but are unable to identify the offenders, who spoke with their backs to the camera. But their voices have been recorded. Their voices are tinged with dialect. There are linguists who specialize in dialects. One of these is willing, in the interest of national security, to compare the recorded voices with tapes of every conceivable dialect and narrow them down to a particular lo-

*Trans. Richard and Clara Winston (New York: Helen and Kurt Wolff Books / Harcourt Brace Jovanovich, 1980). (German title: *Versuchte Nähe.*) —Ed.

cality. Once that is done, the police have no difficulty in picking out the two offenders from among the citizens of that locality known to have visited Prague, and questioning them until they confess.

I quote the eighth section of Schädlich's story:

A sham briefcase passes through the entrance to the Institute for the National Language. Seven lockers in a lower corner, innocently filled by scholarly lovers of the mother tongue with the result of extensive collecting, at once become seven factors of state security. On fifteen hundred tapes in seven lockers are present the northern, eastern, western, and central idiosyncrasies of the language of the divided country.

Official hands press the catches of the briefcase lock. Thumb and forefingers of the right hand produce, from portable custody, a tape, two captive voices.

Appropriate technology induces the voices to repeat dissident opinions; the peculiarities of their speech identify them as inhabitants of a region.

Which one?

Two out of three available experts in the native tongue yield no information despite friendly, friendly and monitory, then insistent urging.

A third expert and the official open a map of the accessible nation, exchange professional opinions on the location of the desired region, and use a blue felt pen to complete an encirclement. They open lockers full of perishable speech, comb the encircled area sector by sector, following the tapes in their slipcases; they compare their specimens with the fragments of native speech that the one-half of the nation readily offered for preservation; they reject, confirm the general direction of their undertaking, and relentlessly approach the inhabitants of a single region.

Of this region here. More specifically, of this administrative district.

At the very beginning of Franz Kafka's novel *The Castle* the one and only technical appliance found in the impoverished village is a telephone.

That's as far as progress had gone at the turn of the century. By 1968 the bureaucracy had learned to make use of television and tape recorders. Since then further progress has been made on both sides of the Iron Curtain. The surveyor K. must keep abreast of developments. The Castle is never behindhand.

RACING WITH
THE UTOPIAS

First published in Die Zeit, *June 16, 1978.*

The human head is bigger than the globe. It conceives itself as containing more. It can think and rethink itself and ourselves from any desired point outside the gravitational pull of the earth. It starts by writing one thing and later reads itself as something else. The human head is monstrous.

Hence our hubris. That is why, unlike all other animals (including birds), we point beyond ourselves. And so our head-born progress reaches out beyond us. Chasing a happiness that is far outside us, we wander small-mindedly through spacious head-systems; for man should always be more than his aptitudes promise. Because too much is asked of him, he asks too much of himself. He always has to reach out beyond himself in search of a better world beyond his allotted years, even before its time is ripe.

As long as human beings have been on the move—and they have been searching longer than we have records of their existence—they have tried to catch up with their utopia; this can amount to a petit-bourgeois idyll of total welfare, flowery trimmings, or it can be the kingdom of God. For centuries it was situated outside this vale of tears; then men began looking for paradise on earth. No, several paradises, for one was not big enough to encompass so many different conceptions of justice, freedom, faith, order, and security. Enough was never enough.

And so, with his big head that transcends the world, man imagines. And what he imagines becomes reality for him, because it is imaginable, thinkable; more real than the sharp corners on which he daily barks his shins. He wants to know, and knows in advance, what lies in the wild blue yonder. He speaks with assurance of a tangible utopia. He looks for it everywhere, even when planting vegetables. And just as the motorcar is thought to be an advance over the horse and buggy, so Cézanne is supposed to represent progress beyond Raphael. What is must always be better than what was, and that which is to come must be better than what is and what was. Even the conservative saying that things used to be better—they can only get worse—is just a reversal of this monstrous thinking beyond the present.

Thus the Promethean head gives us no peace. It calls its searching, roaming restlessness, forever starting out on utopian trails, creative. The new engenders the new. And because man is never satisfied with what he has accomplished, and because nothing can be built on clouds, for some time now new and bigger things have been done in the heart of nature through the leashing or controlled unleashing of, or by outright attacks on, nature: inorganic synthetics and the already achieved utopia of nuclear energy by fission.

In recent years new inventions (and new offshoots of new inventions) have been developed outside earthbound nature: satellites, space stations circle around us, or leave us to visit other planets and come back, bringing knowledge that will continue the process of enabling oversized heads to conceive something new.

For instance, because UFOs are thinkable, they also exist and are beginning to visit us, in films and in reality. The new conception of God has already taken on the shape of a saucer. Once again salvation or perdition is expected from outside. A new type of astral archangel is now on the drawing board. Release from this earthly vale of tears is expected from cosmic space. Only the utopia presented in the Apocalypse of Saint John raises difficulties, because it's hard to beat; and old records must be beaten at all costs. If a present-day Heinrich Schütz were to frame the present yearning for redemption from our over-populated vale of tears, his music would have to sound even more disembodied and ethereal than Schütz's starving choirs did in the days of the Thirty Years' War. That must be feasible. At last we can make the ether sing. At last there's a prospect of winning—in pictures at least—our race with all the utopias that were ever thought up by oversized heads. Already there are movies that have caught up with and commercialized our latest and next-to-latest utopias. And so by families, in couples, or all by ourselves we go to the movies to see our future. And those of us who don't care for the movies because even the utopian sort are usually abridged can open books. For we can still read, though harassing schedules make it harder and harder to concentrate, and though our awareness that reading is old-fashioned and a needless waste of time makes us feel more and more foolish. However, the libraries are still open; reading is still, within certain limits, allowed; and books—especially dusty ones—still exert their lure.

Mountains, Oceans, and Giants is the title of Alfred Döblin's great, excessive, forgotten novel, which appeared in 1924 and needs to be rediscovered: a blueprint of the future written immediately after the author's Wallenstein novel, which suggests a future in backward flight. This book does not, like science fiction, draw on existing technologies, but takes potential and barely conceivable technologies for granted. The major parts of the narrative were written in a burst of visionary exaltation; its flights of ideas, chains of images, eruptions of emotion are at once realistic and diffuse; they fester, abscess, then suddenly subside, flooded by imaginary action.

In *Mountains, Oceans, and Giants* we meet up with people who have deserted the countryside for enormous megalopolises; naturally, as it were, not just figuratively, their sickly bodies—inactive for generations, since no physical effort is required of them and they are fed carefully calculated rations of synthetic Meki Food—grow gigantic heads. Is this the future? Döblin writes retrospectively of the mid-twenty-sixth century: "Physicists and chemists emancipated themselves from plants and animals. The thought that a single dry summer could condemn whole regions to starvation had long inspired amusement mingled with disgust; how absurd to be so dependent on the climate. There was nothing those chemists hated so much as golden wheat fields, meadows, and those preposterous herds of cattle. . . ."

Shortly thereafter, in the narrator's past tense, we are given the following news of the future: "People moved back into the giant cities. They encapsulated themselves in the cities, leaving the largest part of the earth uninhabited. The soil rested. . . ." And farther on: "The harsh, passionate struggle of the workers ceased. From then on, the Western population was almost totally engulfed by enormous cities and divided into a small body of the active and the enormous mass of the inactive. People shifted from one group to the other according to need or inclination. The idle increased in number, and it became necessary to keep them busy with amusements and ostensible work. The once homogeneous racial stock degenerated quickly. A chaotic multiplicity developed. The rulers were assisted by pseudo-parliaments and large staffs of experts, whose task it was to divert the idle masses."

Small wonder that a society structured in this way, which, phony parliaments and all, will probably be with us sooner than Döblin foresaw, can always think up ideas that never occurred to anyone before, and that what it thinks up becomes reality. Witness the great supracontinental Western and Asian empires; the Uralian War between them, in which the contenders manipulate the elements; the temporary exodus from the cities, the great male-eating women's societies, the deglaciation of Greenland, and other miraculous horrors, all of which, in random variations, will have a future, thanks to oversized human heads. And so it goes up to page 511 of my edition of *Mountains, Oceans, and Giants,* when the Giants are defeated and the head's last destructive frenzy dissolves into Veneska, the primal mother principle: "Black the ether above them, dotted with minuscule suns, clusters of stars, sparkling as they turned to slag. The blackness lay breast to breast with the sons of man; light shone from them."

I took this excessive book about man's heaven-storming excesses with me and read it by way of comparison on a recent trip to Asia and Africa, where all these utopias—the past, the retrospective, those that have already been overtaken, those that have failed, and those that are not yet on the program—are today exemplified.

It is not true that utopianism feeds exclusively on the synthetic foods of the future. What it ate in the past it excretes in the present to satisfy its future hunger. In Japan—my first stop—I saw one of Döblin's megalopolises, the Kyoto-Osaka-Kobe area, compared with which the Ruhr Valley is a pleasure resort framed in green. From the harbors to the old imperial city on the heights, this whole area may be described as a ravaged plain, reaching out to the horizon and occupied by hovels and skyscrapers, building sites, demolished buildings, self-contained industrial compounds, scrap heaps, forgotten rice fields. Everything merges with everything else. The tiny, traditionally stylized rock gardens with sprawling heaps of industrial waste that spill over into cemeteries. Over there, where the ancestor cult, the last remnant of picture-book Japan, is impressively preserved in hewn stone, it is protected by blind corners of the railroad line leading to the not-very-distant Greater Tokyo area; three hours by fast train through a thickly settled region, past Nagoya, a city of millions, beyond which terraced rice fields and seed beds covered with plastic wrap try to tell us that—if only in a very limited area—some vestiges of nature are still left.

Soon whole regions will have become megalopolises. The only countryside left will be deserts or nature parks. And at some time or other—in the West right now, in Döblin's book not beginning till page 229—the cities overflow. But where will they overflow to in Japan, where not a parcel of land lies fallow and the sea is never more than two steps away? All this hard work, this rice-and-fish frugality, this complex smile, this repressed desire for continental living space, this already unchained capacity for supplying the markets of the world with gadgets and accessories—where is this country, once defeated in war, now peacefully plying its profitable trades, this still, or once again, leading Asian power—where is it to overflow to?

In Japan's department stores, which are jam-packed like those everywhere else, Japanese people who look Japanese move about among long-legged mannekins that have rosy complexions, are dressed in Western style, and embody the white race. That's what the Japanese want to be like. No more slit eyes for them; what they want is big blue doll's eyes out of which to look down on all diminutive people. Where the cool blond giants come from: that's where they want to go when their cities overflow. For overflow they will, and sooner than Alfred Döblin foresaw.

Sick of freedom from work, disgusted with idleness and their daily ration of Meki Food, no longer willing to carry their oversized heads on frail bodies, the masses escape from the cities. In hordes they move out to the country and amuse themselves looking for a past utopia. Then new Asian, African megalopolises spread; their masses mix with Western nomadic hordes and overrun the continental steppes. Like a sponge, Europe absorbs the overflowing peoples.

The people of Japan are still sticking it out on their islands, those overloaded ships. They still put up with living shoulder to shoulder, in serried rows and layers like the billions of dried salt fish one sees in Japanese markets, arranged according to size and species, spitted on poles or crated and ready for export. They exploit the seas, not only in their own backyard, but also at the ends of the earth. Fish, mollusks, seaweed, eel grass, sea cucumbers, Arctic kelp, anything that can be dried, pressed, packed in rows and layers, condensed into fish concentrate, or ground into fish meal, is brought in, and might suffice to feed the world until the seas are exhausted. The Japanese should be admitted everywhere; they would come with their know-how and their fish. Already they have started eel-grass plantations out at sea. Already they lead the world in breeding fish. Already they make dark-green sheets of gelatin from seaweed, stamp it into squares of any required size, seal it in plastic wrap, and store it indefinitely—say, until the year 2000.

If all this marine produce were used to compensate for the world's shortages, and if the Japanese, who find a use for everything, were given exclusive license to exploit the Seven Seas, the world's food problem would at last be solved and one more utopia would be domesticated. And in among the vendors of sea foods, I saw shops selling gadgets of various kinds, some no larger than a fingernail, instruments of whose functioning I know nothing, but which, because they can be produced cheaply thanks to low wages, might, like dried algae, supply the world with popular-priced data banks, family-sized computers, and other cute toys, as long as the world markets remain open.

And in between, nothing. To one side, the mass products of nature, smelling like fish; on the other, the latest technological whimsies, smelling like nothing at all. Between them a hole. An utter vacuum. For between fish and electronics, the Japanese are jiggling marionettelike on the vestigial strings of surviving traditions and in the tangled web of present-day neuroses. Peaceful, except for the instances of terrorism and counterterrorism to be found everywhere else. And at the same time industrious, punctual. With so much aggressive past and repression-saturated present in common, the Germans and the Japanese might do a lively trade in national clichés. They are said to be comparable, though the Japanese allegedly present a constitutional anomaly: inability to digest milk products. Both peoples are said to repent of their sins and to have become so thoroughly democratic that they have stopped persecuting their minorities, a contention that seems all the more credible since there are virtually no Jews left in Germany, while in Japan the *eta*—or unclean—are today more or less tolerated.

There seem to be two or three million of them. Information is hard to come by, and what answers one gets are whispered from behind a shielding hand. In ancient times the Japanese ate meat and were able to digest milk products. In the sixth century, when the Buddhists took over and outlawed killing, the new doctrine was interpreted restrictively as applying only to the slaughtering of cattle; the eating of meat was regarded as unclean. People even got out of the habit of eating milk products. Since then slaughterers, butchers, tanners, and shoemakers have been looked upon with loathing. They are called *eta*. They exist throughout Japan, concentrated in villages or thinly scattered, most frequently in the country around Kyoto, Osaka, and Hiroshima. Though not persecuted, they are all discriminated against. Carefully as they conceal their origin, one day it comes out that they are *eta*. Whereupon they lose their professional, and with it their social, status and find themselves going downhill in a land of upward mobility. In modern Japan, as everywhere else, there is of course a movement for the defense of minorities. The parliament includes socialist and communist members belonging to the *eta* class, but for the present they are fighting among themselves (ideological battles, it goes without saying).

I was almost glad to find minority problems in a country so well balanced (almost to the point of uniformity) as Japan; for all our present-day populations—unlike Döblin's future masses, who have left all racial distinctions behind them—are riddled with minorities. In Japan it's unclean meat-eaters who are able to digest milk products. The Jews of Indonesia are the able Chinese, who promote commerce of every kind but also lend money at usurious interest. In 1966, in the terrible purge that followed the fall of Sukarno, two to four hundred thousand people were killed out of fear of the Communists and on the pretext of a Communist peril, among them many thousand Chinese, who were suspected of Communism because they were good at business and invested their capital profitably. And in East Africa, which I visited on the last leg of my trip, it is the Indians who replace the Japanese *eta* or the Indonesian Chinese in the role of Jews. In Uganda, Idi Amin showed the world how to handle minorities. You need them because, if kept under adequate pressure, they keep the economy going; you kill them because they are the indispensable internal enemy; but because you can't manage without this internal enemy, you spare a small fraction of them.

Oh, the beautiful Third World! Indonesia is a rich, green, luxuriant, poor country, blessed with three annual rice harvests. First bled white by the Dutch, it is now plagued with indigenous corruption. A third of the rice it needs must be imported, whereas the similarly rice-eating Japanese, in the midst of industrial waste and without the blessing of three harvests, produce more rice than they need and export it.

Ventilators, bicycles, motorcycles, cameras, all the technological gadgets that man dreams up to multiply his needs—almost all come from Japan, Hong Kong, Singapore, the three dominant megalopolises, whose production centers tower into the twenty-first century while slums fester, the Middle Ages linger on, and the fear of demons endures at the foot of their glass fronts, which reflect one another. Cheap goods, contraband, circulates through the channels of corruption, for no other goods are available. And because bribery, practiced throughout the world by Siemens, Unilever, and their fellows, is customary in Indonesia and opens all doors, the Japanese are allowed to fell the last rare-wood forests in distant Borneo, and so intensively that not a ray of hope is left for the ecologists' dreams of reforestation. With the help of official corruption they will soon have obtained deep-sea fishing rights in the seas of Indonesia, for the rulers of Indonesia are so excessively concerned with preserving their power, sinecures, and swelling Swiss bank accounts that they have no time to do what is so obviously needed for the other 120 million Indonesians, eighty million of whom are living packed like sardines in Java and multiplying, no time to develop the pathetic coastal fisheries into a deep-sea fishing industry which, with the help of a refrigeration system—provided by Siemens perhaps (why not?)—might supply the whole population with fish.

But Siemens is thinking of quicker profits, and the deep-sea fishing industry is being left to the Japanese. They have the know-how. They are not only capable of producing hundreds of thousands of motorcycles; they also know that everything—that is, survival, the future—depends on fish and other products of the sea.

But we haven't yet gone as far as Alfred Döblin did in his futurist brainstorms. There are still no Meki factories providing the megalopolises and slums of the entire world with synthetic food, free of charge. Or perhaps we have progressed to that point but are holding back this crucial invention, as, according to Döblin, the senates of the English megalopolises did. They threw Meki, a wise cynic who lived only for his invention, into jail and kept him there for ten years, until he killed himself: "London saw it was imperative to gain exclusive possession of all the secrets of synthesis and of the entire productive process; it realized that this would provide an unparalleled instrument of power."

In Döblin's book, the European oversized heads gain world supremacy through their monopoly on Meki Food. After his death they put up monuments to the suicide Meki. But in my opinion it's the Japanese who will lead in this field. They are so quiet, so politely persistent. They've adapted their gift for destructive, self-destructive Kamikaze offensives to peacetime goals. Gently, not noisily like the American show-offs, modestly, without the arrogance of the European big wheels, they will slip in their innovations; while continuing to dominate the market for motorcycles, photographic equipment, minicomputers, and dried fish, the Japanese Meki manufacturers will float their first stock issues. The turnover is still negligible, almost absurdly so—we've read about all that in a thick tome about the future; Döblin was the author's name—but the demand is on the increase, provoked by curiosity among the jaded, by hunger among the masses.

Because hunger is on the increase. Everything else may be stagnating. Every step forward may turn out to be a step backward. In Europe there may be more and more senior citizens while schoolhouses stand empty, because at some time or other too few children were begotten. But in Asia the Pill hasn't made a dent in the birthrate; children are everywhere, in the slums, in the villages. Beautiful children, cheerful children. Quiet, undernourished children, eagerly looking forward to producing more children, because children make for a bustling, meaningful life, because procreating is something even the poorest of the poor can do, because swarms of children are a substitute for social security and none of the people in power would dream of replacing this poor-man's social-security system—based on a plentiful supply of children—with a government-operated system. Because that would be socialism. And socialism—as even our European demagogues know—leads straight to communism.

That—and not because God has willed it—is why the only real growth today is provided by the population explosion, which is indeed an explosion and results in increasing unemployment, poverty, undernourishment, epidemics, and hunger. And were it not that the Japanese (who in Döblin's book are the English) will soon be capable of supplying mankind, not only with low-priced computers and worldwide data-bank systems, but also with synthetic Meki Food, there would really be cause for despair, because nothing else functions.

That's how writers talk. In their books, the action continues. When the Meki factories had appeased the world's hunger with synthetic food, men began, because they were kept in a state of sated inactivity, to grow flabby and to lose interest in themselves. "Suddenly," writes author Döblin, "a dangerous indifference set in, spreading decay.... After that, pomp, games, and feasting had little effect. Confronted with machine-made objects that were fashionable, life-stimulating, stunningly beautiful, people stood silent with sagging jaws. They began to rummage about for old, forgotten costumes."

To counter this slackness and dangerous retrospection, the industry-dominated senates of the Western megalopolises unleashed the Uralian War. When, carrying the Western and Eastern masses with them, its fire storms had devoured one another and peace set in, daily feedings of Meki Food were thought to be the wave of the future. Then the megalopolises overflowed. People fled from those who controlled the long-range and short-range machines. Settler movements destabilized the whole world. Old farm implements were dug up. Shamans, the so-called Deceivers, preached Back to Nature. So once again the oversized heads had to think up something new, a new mission for mankind. The next project was the deglaciation of Greenland, a superhuman disaster, unleashing the fury of nature, yet accomplished without that nuclear energy which our oversized heads have devised for future utopias and present disasters.

Never fear, something will survive. Even in *Mountains, Oceans, and Giants* there are survivors, though reduced to archaic dimensions and with smaller heads. Döblin's future is in general quite different from ours. No star wars. No astral beings of a third kind to haunt us. Everything stays where it belongs on its earthly carpet, which is pulled out from under mankind, sometimes slowly, as though on rational grounds, but sometimes so brusquely that we stumble. And the latest technologies, if they exist at all, are barely hinted at, haphazardly sketched in. No details are worked out and made technically credible. Even the Meki factories are a mere hypothesis. In the Uralian War and other classic attempts at resolving contradictions, long-distance ray guns, termed "mechanisms" for short, are spoken of only in passing. The deglaciation of Greenland, that enormous spectacle, is made possible by tourmaline screens, the energy for which has been obtained by blowing up the volcanoes of Iceland for this very purpose. Döblin states this, and behold, it becomes fact—as credible as the fact that there are no writers in his future world of *Mountains, Oceans, and Giants*.

They are absent from the start. No one writes and no one gets published. Since no one reads, no forbidden books are confiscated. Just once, when Meki Food had induced general asthenia and dangerous retrospection, we read: "Germans held their heavy Bibles in their hands, thumbed through hymn books, sang gloomily in the woods." No other literary reference. And because, despite all the violence and counterviolence, despite all the individual and mass destruction, not a single writer is arrested, no writers have to protest against the arrest or banishment of writers. Taking the long view, Döblin jumped over his existence as an author, the burning of the books, his exile during the Nazi period. As though his profession had no future.

But we haven't got to that point. Not yet. In Japan, Hong Kong, Indonesia, Thailand, India, and Kenya, in all the countries I went to—and lectured in accordance with the program of the Goethe Institute—there are writers, that is, persons who, in a hesitant, old-fashioned sort of way, which no technology can speed up, make words, form sentences, and nudge the various conflicting realities into a new, fictitious (i.e., literary) reality. A dangerous profession, because extra-literary realities and their custodians usually see themselves in political terms—in other words, as exclusive. They refuse to recognize any reality besides their own, not even a fictitious one. So it comes about that wherever only one reality is in force the authorities silence writers by censoring, suppressing, and confiscating their books, by driving them out of the country, arresting them, or removing them from every reality once and for all.

That is what happened in Indonesia more than twelve years ago to the writer Pramudya Ananta Toer, whose books deal with the narrow world of landless peasants oppressed by usury and corruption. Reason enough for Sukarno's successors to lock him up along with thousands of others in an island concentration camp. For twelve years he was neither brought to trial nor amnestied. All appeals and petitions in his favor went unheard. Since their overriding interest is in holding on to their power, the military rulers of Indonesia are afraid of writers, and in this they are not alone: they have plenty of company.

Where I come from—the twofold Germany—and where I went on my trip—to Thailand and Kenya, for instance—the rulers have always known, or have quickly learned, how to deal with writers. No need to talk about the German Democratic Republic; its methods are common knowledge. On the other hand, it is becoming increasingly evident that the West German snooping system is encouraging a depressing development that has its traditions in Germany and is taken up by the countries of the Third World the moment they gain their independence.

Since early this year, the Kikuyu writer Ngugi Wa Thiong'o has been imprisoned in an unknown locality.* The rulers in Nairobi are indifferent to the fact that such abuse of power is in no way distinguishable from the current practice in South Africa, Czechoslovakia, Chile, and the Soviet Union. In their ways of dealing with people who see, imagine, or even, as in the case of writers, write about other realities outside or alongside the prescribed reality, the ideologies have become very much alike. Their need for security accounts for this rapprochement. Hostile and mutually exclusive as the capitalist and communist systems purport to be, when it comes to safeguarding their internal security they are one in their abuse of power.

Because I am a writer, it is the effect of this diabolical harmony on the fate of writers that strikes me first of all; it is equally evident that hundreds of thousands of nonwriters owe their banishment, arrest, and often enough their death to the same ideological convergence.

But writers are the most suitable targets. They are frightening, because of their old-fashioned self-sufficiency. They subsist

*He has since been released. —ED.

on next to nothing: a bit of paper. They live on contradictions. What they think up takes form, makes itself independent, and acts without incurring legal responsibility. That won't do. It disturbs the peace, endangers security, promotes radicalism, obstructs progress, raises questions when what we need is answers: clear-cut, practical answers, relevant to the present situation, and don't forget it!

That's why there are no writers in *Mountains, Oceans, and Giants*. In Döblin, mankind has gone further. The great convergence of prevailing ideologies, developed in the present era, has no need of writers, not even as ornaments; either these troublesome questioners were got rid of long ago, or else they survive but have stopped writing; marginal dreamers, they have given up trying to say anything and consume themselves for want of a medium of communication. All that's left is a literature lived and practiced without benefit of proof sheets. Consider the strange Jonathan, for instance.

His mother was a member of the new ruling class, the technological aristocracy. Though after the Uralian War the consuls Marke and Marduk, the absolute rulers of the megalopolis Berlin, prohibited all scientific research, she worked secretly in a group that had set itself the task of increasing the supply of synthetic food, with the help of accelerated growth processes. The consul Marduk had once belonged to this group but had then broken with it and decreed radical regression; he had even wanted to abolish the old, established Meki Food, but there was simply not enough farm or pasture land in the hopelessly over-populated megalopolis between the Oder and the Elbe.

In the course of a purge, Marduk had twenty-one scientists, among them Jonathan's mother, arrested and shut up in an experimental forest, the trees and bushes of which proceeded to swell and proliferate and exude juices until the forest absorbed the bodies of the scientists. A synthetic natural substance, as it were, entered into ever new combinations, with the result that the inventors of the growth miracle dissolved in their invention: "The mammothlike, oozing, crashing growth squeezed, pressed, mangled the scientists, crushed their rib cages, broke their backbones, compressed their skulls, poured their white brains over the roots. . . . The tree trunks mingled. . . ." And farther on: "Marduk pressed his oversized head to the window: 'It's all over. You can't do anything now.' "

The boy Jonathan becomes the favorite of the power-mad Marduk and of a series of women, the domineering leaders of women's societies, who combat male rule but are no less power-hungry than their male counterparts. Time and again the battle between the sexes surges up, and through it staggers the sensitive and unhappy Jonathan, never definitely committed to either camp. As a sensitive yet inexpressive individual, he is the embodiment of the writer who no longer writes, a plaything of the powerful, whose arsenal of terror fuses the techniques of our present-day system, just as the experimental forest fused its inventors.

In Döblin's *Mountains, Oceans, and Giants,* as in George Orwell's apocalyptic *1984,* all the superficially hostile ideologies of today have coalesced. In the global power system of Orwell's oligarchical collectivism, fascist and Stalinist structures are one. No longer identifiable by antithetical emblems, both together, effecting a synthesis of the two power structures, operate the great, all-encompassing data bank. And this view of the future is also that of Döblin's novel. In both books, our present capitalist and communist social systems, with their subordinate clerico-fascist and semicommunist military regimes, have gone out of existence. And so have such notions as democracy, liberalism, worker management, and democratic socialism; or, rather, they have become unrecognizable, having been fused into a single total, all-controlling power structure, whose accumulated aggressions explode now and then without the ideological justifications still current today, in continental wars, regional pacification campaigns, and occasional wars between the sexes.

True, we still talk about humanism, we still parrot the

achievements of the European Enlightenment and the ethical values of Christianity, we still invoke the rights of the individual, human rights in general, and the right to work. But the future reality, described in advance by Döblin and later by Orwell, has already begun, and it seems likely that the systems they had in mind will be achieved sooner than the prophets foresaw.

Whether in Asia or Africa, none of the established power systems, and none of those now establishing themselves by putsches of one sort or another, can be clearly defined in terms of traditional ideologies. Everywhere we find instead the oligarchical collectivism which Orwell predicted for 1984 and which Döblin foresaw as the system of power and control prevailing in his megalopolises. In Indonesia or Thailand the ruling classes happen to be anticommunist and therefore totalitarian, whereas the rulers of Burma and Cambodia define themselves as socialist and justify their totalitarian rule on grounds of anticapitalism and anti-imperialism. But regardless of interchangeable ideological costumes and the permutations of their ruling classes, all these states have one thing in common: they are all being absorbed by a worldwide collectivism, whose technological superstructure, from data banks to nuclear reactors, is being supplied, in free imitation of Döblin and Orwell, by the industrial countries of both blocks.

Small wonder that in so present a future writers should become touching anachronisms, reeling between the holders of power. True, they still write; true, their appeals and protests still ring, as they have always done, with the pathos of humanism; true, the authorities on both sides, overestimating their dangerousness, lock them up, banish them to islands, deport them, or try—as was done to my colleague Hochhuth—to silence them by court order; true, the authorities still need them marginally and offer prizes and grants to encourage what is elsewhere a penal offense; true, just about everywhere the powers-that-be behave as if they mean to preserve this endangered species just a little longer. Yet it is quite obvious why writers can no longer express themselves in Döblin's future reality; like Jonathan, they have ceased to be anything more than emotional wrecks, impoverished relics without paper.

But even thus reduced, they are in the way. Like troublesome ghosts they haunt the megalopolises, and their emotional force, which burns all the more brightly for lack of expression, is looked upon as an irritant. They radiate playful tenderness, overflowing sympathy, nostalgia for a past that would like to dream up a future, old-fashioned brotherly love. In the midst of unfeeling power struggles, they preserve their sensibility. No terror deters them from communicating their thoughts and feelings. In the midst of slum areas encompassing all the misery of this world, of regions afflicted by drought, drained of their last resources by government-sponsored corruption—wherever injustice is silent to high heaven, I saw Jonathan at work. Man or woman. He has no gender. He is active feeling, unrelated to utility or success—and no doubt a mirror image of Döblin, who tended the poor in Berlin's Urban-Krankenhaus.

In Thailand he is a young doctor who runs a ten-bed hospital in the northwestern district of Prathai, a province afflicted by drought and starvation. At first sight one would take him for a boy—he's twenty-eight—with the cheerful smile usual among the Thais. I saw him going about his well-nigh-hopeless task with concentration—he's the only doctor in a district of eighty thousand inhabitants. Epidemics, tuberculosis, belated pleas for sterilization, undernourishment, malnutrition and its resulting diseases are the substance of his working day. The region is dominated by a few wealthy landowners, who employ armed gangs to seize the last water buffaloes of the impoverished peasants. The police side with the landowners. The doctor knows it and is helpless. He has opted for the undernourished, worm-infested children.

Matter-of-factly, as though wishing to corroborate his regional statistics, he listed the causes—an unbalanced rice diet, lack of vitamins B_1, B_2, and A, shortage of protein—and showed me the symptoms: brittle, lusterless hair, eye diseases, inflammation at the corners of the mouth, rashes, bloated bellies. To combat the terror of the gangs and the corruption at the base of the state he would have to leave the children and the sick and go into the jungle, where the resistance is building up. This doctor has decided to stay where he is as long as they let him.

There used to be forests here; they were cut down in the heedless manner usual in this part of the world. Since then, we are told, there has been no rainfall even in the monsoon season. The doctor is unable to move the seriously ill; there's no ambulance. Power failure is a feature of everyday life. The doctor's pay is negligible. What makes him stick it out in this hospital without water? He's an exception. In the neighboring districts there are no doctors. He was born in Prathai, studied in Bangkok, then returned to his district. Bangkok is saturated with doctors. None wants to work in the country, in the drought areas. They all want to stay in the cities; their dream is to set up a practice in Europe or America.

Why do I write about this isolated doctor? Because I want to set him off against thousands of Asian and African doctors, who study in Europe or America, stay there, and never go back to their provinces. Doctors on paper, they are lost to their countries. Many claim the right of asylum, when what they've actually done is run out on their jobs. This one doctor discredits them all. Their refusal should be measured by his conduct. They should be shamed by his example, but I'm afraid they only laugh at him.

In Khlong Toei, the enormous Bangkok waterfront slum, I saw a young woman who might have been the sister of the doctor in Prathai. Born and raised there, she became a teacher but nevertheless has stayed in the slums. She teaches unregistered children, who, because they are not registered, are not admitted to the public schools. Khlong Toei is a jumble of shacks perched on stilts planted in a swamp gorged with garbage and excrement, which swells during the monsoon rains and floods the gangways between the shacks. Sixty thousand people live there, including eight thousand children. The teacher is able to help barely a hundred of them. Every day she gives each of them a bowl of diluted soya milk. The soya milk is provided by Terre des Hommes, which also supplies the doctor in Prathai with medicines.

These are drops in the bucket, but they count. For all their hopelessness, the doctor's work and the slum school (with its soya milk) strike me as more real and more honest than any number of impressive development projects, whose resources are in large part drained off into administrative channels and whose ostentatious results only accentuate the poverty of the undeveloped regions in which they are situated. These "achievements" include a steel mill, a semiautomatic fertilizer plant, a superclinic, and even, in Djakarta, a photo-composition printing plant, which, however, does not print schoolbooks as originally planned, but concentrates on pictorial wrapping paper. Of course the paper has to be imported, because, rather than take the trouble to build up an Indonesian paper industry, the authorities preferred to put the cart before the horse and (with the help of tax-privileged capital supplied by West German and Dutch publishers) put up an unneeded printing plant, which, to show a profit, grinds out wrapping paper that only makes shopping more expensive in an impoverished country.

Better Terre des Hommes and its many drops in the bucket! This small relief organization, financed by private gifts, supported neither by state nor by church funds, has specialized in the distress of children in the slum districts. Of these there is no lack. For the only really positive growth rate at the present time is that of the world's population, which has its corollaries in the growth of unemployment and undernourishment and the flight of the landless peasants from the drought-and-starvation-plagued provinces to the slums.

Here we see the hallmarks of the future. Here the scenes are staked out for Döblin's mass conflicts. Here in the megalopolises, neighboring worlds are locked in a death struggle—in Bombay, for instance.

Some seventy thousand people are living in the Janatha Colony, which is now called Cheetah Camp, one of the biggest slums in Greater Bombay, of whose seven million inhabitants two or three million are estimated to live in slums. The Indian Centre for Nuclear Research, to which India owes its first atom bomb, was built on the edge of what used to be the Janatha Colony. The nuclear scientists were unhappy about having a slum next door. They spoke of a security risk. So in May 1976 the Janatha Colony was forcibly evacuated and razed with bulldozers. The seventy thousand inhabitants were sent to a new slum, a low-lying tract of land on the ocean front, which becomes a swamp in the rainy season. Several hundred children died in the first months. Suicides were frequent. The Centre for Nuclear Research decided to devote the vacated land to recreational facilities. Now the nuclear scientists can relax on the golf courses or tennis courts, and a swimming pool is projected. They are enjoying their work again. They feel secure among their own kind: the new elite, the owners of oversized heads, capable of thinking beyond the sweating masses and their slum horizon. They are the people who count. They are precious. The future belongs to them.

In *Mountains, Oceans, and Giants*, the scientific elite are identical with the autocratic senates of the megalopolises. They have abolished parliaments or reduced them to travesties of parliaments. The industrialists back them. It was the scientists who defeated the machine wreckers. The findings of their research —and not the sordid needs of the masses—point the way. They have put an end to laborious farming and to the servitude of full employment by rationalizing the factories and supplying the unemployed masses with synthetic food. When enforced idleness threatened to degenerate into anarchy, scientist-statesmen devised a safety valve: the Uralian War. After the cities overflowed, it was the scientists who chained the restlessly roving masses to a new objective: the deglaciation of Greenland. And when the tourmaline screens had laid Greenland bare down to its Cretaceous strata and raised its vegetation to the boiling point; when gigantic aurochses and flying dragons as long as city blocks broke loose from the all-engulfing growth, left Greenland, and descended on the Western megalopolises, terrifying the masses, it was again the scientists who knew the answer. They entrusted the struggle against the tourmaline-engendered monsters to the so-called tower-people: immense synthetic creatures which, like Marduk's omnivorous synthetic forest in olden times, absorbed animals and humans and were stimulated to gigantic growth by irradiation with tourmaline. And the terrified masses, as well as the laboratories and Meki Food factories, were moved from the surface of the earth to underground megalopolises: "When story after story had been pounded into the clay and larger and larger caverns torn open, when masses of earth and blasted rock had been piled up between the rows of houses on the earth's surface, no one felt afraid any longer. The people did not run away from the monsters. They had embarked on a great new expedition. The senates cried out: 'Get off the earth!' And joyfully the people dug themselves in; now they themselves experienced the miracle of human know-how, which the deglaciators of Greenland had known."

Is this a far-out vision of the future? Even if the deglaciation of Greenland with all its fabulous consequences looks like a grandiose literary horror story, the relocation underground of all or part of mankind—or, alternatively, to giant concentration camps circling the earth on satellites—is conceivable because it is possible and possible because it is conceivable. The disgust and security-mindedness of the Indian nuclear scientists were strong and plausible enough to make the evacuation of the enormous slum district nearby seem reasonable. The present slum of Cheetah Camp is right next door to the arsenal of the Indian navy, and the question of security is again being raised. But where are the slums of Bombay, Calcutta, Hong Kong, Djakarta, Bangkok, or Nairobi to go if their removal and partial rehabilitation results only in larger slums and an accelerated rural exodus? "Underground!" cry the senates of Döblin's megalopolises. "Out into space!" may soon be the recommendation of an international slum-clearance commission.

As it is, the slums are deprived of municipal services; the city's garbage trucks, water supply, sewage system, schools, and hospitals are not for them. Yet, rotting and stinking, they expand, coalesce, and threaten to engulf the city. But there's nowhere to put them—unless the future actually takes its cue from Döblin.

We now know what oversized heads have thought up and are capable of thinking up. Despite loud or tacit protestations to the contrary, it is now generally acknowledged that after us the deluge may indeed come. While the latest inventions are probing the future, our present is being overtaken by the Middle Ages: plagues, fear of demons, diffuse yearnings for redemption, religious mania are on the rise. The President of the United States is not alone in trusting to divine guidance. Not so long ago, several thousand Brahmans met in Central India to offer up a sacrifice to the gods. In the midst of a famine area, food valued at well over a million dollars—rice, milk, and vegetable fat—was burned. "There is no point," said a leading Brahman, "in helping the present victims of cyclones; instead, we should try, by offering up imposing sacrifices, to prevent future cyclones." A contemporary fragment that might have been found in Döblin.

And so my journey ended, but the race between the utopias is still going on. It might be worth mentioning that *Jaws* was being shown in the cinemas of Hong Kong, Djakarta, and Bangkok; that in Japan's luxury hotels, even in the elevators, there is a constant trickle of classical music—Bach, Vivaldi, Purcell; that everywhere, and most colorfully among the poorest of the poor, life is celebrated, if only in the form of cockfights; that there really are demons in Asia; that Germany is not so much as mentioned anywhere in Asia, except on the financial page or the sports section of the newspapers; and that on this quiet, overcrowded continent German tourists don't shout any louder than their French, Dutch, etc., counterparts.

Back home, everybody was wrapped up in himself and his own petty anxieties. All the cantankerous asides and aggressive gestures in word, picture, and deed seem to be directed against the enemy within. If madness is flowery in Asia, in Europe it is ultra-rational. Yet everything is available here—and nicely packaged too; it's just that there's not much future on hand. You have to go looking for it, take your time, start all over again, read.

In my calendar, Alfred Döblin's hundredth birthday was coming up.

WHAT SHALL WE TELL OUR CHILDREN?

First published in L 76, no. 12 (1979).

"When at the end of March it became necessary to evacuate the Central Synagogue on Reitbahn (as per contract), Doubt and his remaining pupils helped to pack the ritual objects, which were soon sent to New York, where they became the Gieldzinski Collection in The Jewish Museum. (In 1966 the scrolls of the Torah were destroyed when fire broke out in the library.)" This passage in my book *From the Diary of a Snail* relates how the Jewish community of Danzig was dispersed in the spring of 1939 and how it had to finance the emigration of its members by selling the synagogues and Jewish cemeteries. "After the contract was signed, the aged synagogue directors and Leopold Schufftan, the cantor of the Central Synagogue, were said to have wept."

Now, forty years later, the treasures of the Danzig synagogue are being exhibited in New York. My reflections on the subject cannot relate to their cultural or historical significance, but must inevitably follow from the consequences of the German crime and from the nature of my literary activity. For the past can never cease to be present to us, and we are still asking ourselves: How could such a thing happen?

We are still without an answer. Thirty-five years after Auschwitz the problem confronting Germans is once more: What shall we tell our children? Or, more precisely: How are parents born after the war, parents who in their childhood were fobbed off with lies, evasions, and half-answers to their questions, to explain to their own children what was done "in the name of the German people" in Auschwitz, Treblinka, and Majdanek? What are they to say of the German guilt that has lived on from generation to generation and must remain forever indelible?

Other peoples have been more fortunate in a dubious sort of way—that is, more forgetful. No one thinks of holding the Russian people responsible for the mass murder committed in the name of the Revolution under Stalin. Relatively few citizens of the United States feel responsible today for the American war crimes committed in Vietnam. England, France, and Holland have successfully forgotten the injustice (whose consequences are still with us) of their colonial regimes. All that is water under the bridge, ancient history, and history goes on.

The Germans alone cannot evade their responsibility. The more inoffensive they try to seem, the greater the dread they inspire in their neighbors. Their economic success cannot conceal the moral vacuum engendered by their incomparable guilt. No amount of talk about the innocence of the Germans who had not yet been born or about the crimes of other peoples can relieve them of their guilt. Others point at them, and they point at themselves. With the same merciless pedantry that tolerated, planned, and carried out the genocide of six million Jews, they go on asking themselves why it happened, and being asked (more urgently with each generation) by their children. As in the Old Testament, guilt lives on and is inherited. In the late 1960s, I, who for years had questioned others—people of my parents' generation—was questioned by my children, then four, eight, and (the twins) twelve years of age. Being children, they asked: What about the children, were they gassed too? Or: Why children? Or they bogged down in technical details: What kind of gas was it? The numbers, the millions, were beyond their understanding. When my older sons asked about the reasons for such horror, their parents lost themselves in talk of complicated historical, social, or religious developments, cited dozens of causes, which when taken together seemed simply absurd. The children's interest shifted to other questions, relating to daily life—the golden hamster, a television program, the next vacation.

Only when I spoke of individual destinies—a flight into death, a flight to Palestine, for example—did I hold the children's attention, though I could not be sure that they heard anything more than an adventure story. I began to write down their questions and my uncertain answers. And since I was kept busy from March 1969 to the following fall with the forthcoming Bundestag elections, my children's questions mingled in my diary with notes on the election campaign to form the basis of the book, *From the Diary of a Snail*, that I was to write some time later. In my book the story of the persecution, expulsion, and destruction of the Danzig Jews runs parallel to a record of present-day political events. It seemed to me that my perception of my native city of Danzig was still clear and vivid enough to provide me with a credible setting for an account of the onset and slow development of the German crime. What happened in Berlin, Leipzig, Nuremberg, Frankfurt, and Düsseldorf also happened in Danzig, though somewhat delayed by Danzig's status as a free city. And all in broad daylight. The same limitless hatred was proclaimed in posters and in shouted slogans. The same cowardly silence on the part of the Christian churches. There too the citizenry adapted to the new situation. There too the people deliberately disenfranchised themselves.

My decision to approach the horror of the "final solution" from the periphery, to follow its development in a place well known to me, derived from an old project of mine, undertaken years before and abandoned as a failure—namely, to complete Heinrich Heine's fragment "The Rabbi of Bacherach."*

*This unfinished story by Heinrich Heine (1797–1856) is available in English translation in *Great Jewish Short Stories*, ed. Saul Bellow (New York: Dell Publishing Co., 1963). The quotations that follow are from this translation. —ED.

Heine's romantic irony had provoked me; I wanted to contradict him. His defeat by so overwhelming a subject had aroused my ambition. Today I know that without the detour through Heine's "Bacherach" I would not have found my way to the Jews of Danzig, through whom I hoped to bring the Jewish community of a medieval Rhenish town back to life and uncover threads of destiny that lay buried beneath the sands of time. Three chapters totaling less than sixty pages are all we possess of "The Rabbi of Bacherach." The tale seems to end in mid-sentence. The author assures his readers in parentheses that the ensuing chapters and the end of the tale were lost through no fault of his. And yet, so often was his work on the manuscript interrupted, so unwieldy and unmanageable did the material become, and so compelling were the arguments against publishing the story as a whole or even the fragment at the time, that Heine busied himself with the material for a full fifteen years. The story of the writing of "The Rabbi" reads like a chronicle of failure.

In the summer of 1824, a year after the Napoleonic Edict of Tolerance was partly revoked in Prussia (whereupon it became possible to deprive Jews of teaching positions in schools and universities), the law student (and author of *Die Harzreise— Travels in the Harz Mountains*), began his preliminary work at the Göttingen Library. He who as a poet subscribed as a matter of principle to "indifferentism," who scorned all positive religion, who looked upon Judaism and Christianity alike as expressions of contempt for humanity, whose sole attachment to his origins consisted in an occasional sentimental impulse (and this in exasperation at the dominance of Christianity), he, the liberal who believed only in reason, began to delve into the history of the Jewish people's millennial sufferings. To his friend Moser he wrote: "I am also immersed in the study of chronicles and especially in *historia judaica.* The latter because of its connection with the 'Rabbi' and perhaps also out of inner need. Very special feelings move me when I leaf through those sorrowful annals; in them I find an abundance of instruction and grief."

At the start of the very first chapter, after the small town of Bacherach is presented in a romantic light and the small Jewish community within its walls introduced, the theme is struck in historical retrospect: "The Great Persecution of the Jews began with the Crusades and raged most grimly about the middle of the fourteenth century, at the end of the Great Plague, which, like any other public disaster, was blamed on the Jews. It was asserted that they had brought down the wrath of God, and that they had poisoned the wells with the aid of the lepers."

Heine tells of hordes of medieval flagellants, who, "chanting a mad song to the Virgin Mary," passed through the Rhineland on their way to southern Germany, murdering Jews by the thousands. He points to the source of the centuries-old lie ". . . that the Jews would steal the consecrated wafer, stabbing it with knives until the blood ran from it, and that they would slay Christian children at their Feast of Passover, in order to use the blood for their nocturnal rite."

With this the tragic theme is announced. For with the Feast of Passover, at which the small Jewish community of Bacherach gathers around Rabbi Abraham, the plot of the still-unfinished story begins. While the Rabbi (then a young man, who had studied in Toledo in Spain, where he had come to take a sympathetic view of Christianity) is conducting the old rites in the great hall of his home, while the silver Sabbath lamp "casts its most festive light on the devoutly merry faces of old and young," while, in other words, the liberation of the people of Israel from Egyptian bondage is being peacefully commemorated, adorned with legends, documented from Scripture, and celebrated with the words of the Haggadah—"Behold, this is the food our fathers ate in Egypt! Let any who is hungry come and partake!"—two strange men in wide cloaks enter the hall and present themselves as traveling coreligionists who wish to join in the Passover service.

As grandly as the celebration is described—"the men sat in their black cloaks and black, flat hats and white ruffs; the women in strangely glittering garments made of cloths from

Lombardy, wore their diadems and necklaces of gold and pearls"—the reader is left with a foreboding of doom. A little later, Rabbi Abraham discovers that one of the strangers had brought in the bloody corpse of a child and deposited it under the table—the pretext for the massacre to come. But Heine spares his delicate readers the details of the pogrom, and the story takes a romantic turn. In obedience to the ancient injunction to live and bear witness, the Rabbi leaves his congregation, over whom "the Angel of Death" is hovering, and manages to escape with his young wife, Sarah. They board a boat on the River Rhine, and during the night "Silent Wilhelm who, although a deaf-mute, was a handsome lad," rows them to Frankfurt-am-Main. The two remaining chapters are set in the Frankfurt ghetto. There is no pronounced climax as in the first chapter.

Of the second part of the tale—which was to take place in Spain, as we learn from Heine's letters—we know nothing. He probably chose Spain as the goal of Rabbi Abraham's flight because of the opportunity it would provide to develop his ideal of a tolerance embracing all religions (and his critique of all orthodox doctrines).

Shortly before his graduation in June 1825, Heinrich Heine was baptized as a Protestant. He wished to lecture on philosophy and history in Berlin and also had social ambitions. Yet, though he adapted himself to the servitudes of the day, he continued to work on "The Rabbi of Bacherach" until new interruptions relieved him of a task that was becoming increasingly burdensome. For a time he planned to publish a short version in the second part of his *Reisebilder (Travel Scenes)*, but that too was abandoned. In 1833, when a fire in his mother's house in Hamburg destroyed a large part of the manuscripts stored there, the manuscript of "The Rabbi," which in the meantime had swollen to two volumes, was lost. All that remained were fragmentary rough drafts, with which the author, then an exile in Paris, planned to go on working.

But it was not until 1840 that a current happening—a Passover that ended in a pogrom—led Heine to resume work on his book: a group of Damascus Jews, accused of murdering a Capuchin priest and drinking his blood at their Passover celebration, were tortured by order of Count Ratti-Menton, the French consul. What in Heine's tale had resulted from the superstitious madness of the Middle Ages had been re-enacted in Heine's own time, in defiance of all enlightenment and the humanitarian principles of the French Revolution.

Heine stated his views in a series of articles, some of which appeared in the *Augsburger Allgemeine Zeitung*. In one article suppressed by the editors, he directly attacked the French Prime Minister: "At his morning audience Monsieur Thiers . . . with an air of total conviction, declares it to be an acknowledged fact that the Jews drink Christian blood at their Feast of Passover. . . ."

This series of articles, later collected in the first part of his *Lutetia*, were among Heine's journalistic masterpieces. Tempering the earnestness and passion of his attacks with irony, concealing his grief and shame with wit, digressing to report the latest gossip of the Opéra and draw a picture of contemporary Paris (in expectation of the return of Napoleon's body), he nevertheless keeps hold of his central theme. He proves that the martyrdom of the Jews in Damascus was not an isolated reversion to the Dark Ages, but might well be the forerunner of a new and more terrible form of persecution, fomented by Christian hatred. True, there had been protests against Consul Ratti-Menton, who had instigated the pogrom in Damascus and promoted it with rabble-rousing pamphlets, but the prejudice remained. Heine clearly saw and analyzed the explosive situation in the Near East and the false view taken of it in Europe. In this instance the "indifferentism" often deplored by his Jewish friends helped him to keep cool and (as elsewhere, with regard to Marxism) to foresee the crimes of the twentieth century: the shift of the traditional Christian hatred of the Jews into organized racism and anti-Semitism.

As if the events in Damascus had given him new impetus,

Heine now reworked his tale. But though he dedicated "Das Passahfest" ("The Feast of Passover"), as he now called it, to Baroness Betty Rothschild, he soon withdrew it in favor of his earlier version. Possibly to free himself from the theme, undoubtedly to give more weight to the volume containing his so-called "Salon," he included the three now extant chapters of his fragment, which fulfills its high literary aspiration only in the account of the Passover and otherwise loses itself in flowery descriptions and strained wit.

After fifteen years, Heine tore himself away from the subject that had become an obligation and a burden to him. In his work as a journalist, he gained and communicated clearer insights into the theme. Possibly the failure of the fragment was due to the romantic style of the day, which, even when tempered with irony, was not equal to the terrible reality that Heine was trying, in retrospect and with foreboding, to deal with. In resignation he wrote to Campe, his publisher: "I wrote this picture of medieval life fifteen years ago, and what I am publishing here is only the exposition of the book that was burned in my mother's house—perhaps fortunately for me, since in the latter chapters I reveal heretical views that would have provoked an uproar among Jews and Christians alike."

In a letter to his friend Moser, written before starting work on "The Rabbi," Heine had shown in advance a better appreciation of the provocative quality inherent in the work as it now stands: "I admit that I shall come out vigorously for the rights and civic equality of the Jews, and in the hard times that are sure to come the Germanic mob will hear my voice and responses will be roared in German beer halls and mansions."

There has been a good deal of controversy about Heine, who has usually been approached from the wrong direction. As an enlightened patriot, yet a critic of his country, he was unexcelled. The accuracy of his reporting was termed subversive, his wit denigrated as alien to the German people; still, his flattest rhymes and his self-imitating sentimentalities were numbered among the treasures of German literature, and found quotable at all times. Heine remains a stumbling block to the Germans. His witty seriousness and laughing despair are beyond them. I do not except myself, for when, soon after the end of the war, young and hungry for hitherto forbidden literature, I read Heine's "Rabbi of Bacherach" for the first time, my initial, brief impression was one of annoyance; after that, and for much longer, I saw it as a challenge to embark on a presumptuous venture. I decided to continue the fragment and played (experimentally) with imitations of the style. I wanted the Rhine boatman to carry the fugitives Abraham and Sarah, not to medieval Frankfurt, but to the Frankfurt of the 1930s. A detail at the beginning of the second chapter gave me the idea of continuing the tale in the present. As they approach their destination, Abraham cries out to Sarah: "Over there, those houses beckoning amidst green hills, that's Sachsenhausen, where Lame Gumpertz goes to get the fine myrrh for us at the time of the Feast of Tabernacles. . . ." My leap in time was suggested by this incidental mention of a place that was to give its name to a concentration camp.

An obstinate notion, which kept reviving of its own accord every time I abandoned it as hopeless. But nothing was ever committed to writing, for in the meantime I was pursuing my own ideas. The setting of my story could not be Bacherach, Frankfurt-am-Main (Sachsenhausen), or Toledo. I clung to my roots, and in pursuing my question—How shall I tell my children?—I could only take Danzig as my starting point. The challenge of Heine's fragment was still with me, but it had ceased to be a literary inspiration.

In the mid-1960s, when I went to Israel for the first time, I made the acquaintance in Tel Aviv of Erwin Lichtenstein, who, as a lawyer and former syndic of the Danzig Jewish community, was now busying himself with so-called reparations claims. As a young man, he had been obliged to deal with the Nazi authorities and preside over the sale of Jewish religious buildings and cemeteries. He had collected copious material bearing witness to the persecution, expulsion, and destruction of the Danzig Jews. Although he had been working for years on the manuscript of his book, which was to appear in the early 1970s,* no literary ambition deterred him from putting copies of his documents at my disposal. Through him I was able, on a later trip to Israel, to visit several survivors of the Danzig Jewish community, among them Ruth Rosenbaum, who as a young teacher had founded and directed a Jewish private school, which continued in operation from 1935 to the spring of 1939, in the midst of the rising Nazi terror. Shortly before the "Departure of the Five Hundred" (a shipment of Danzig Jews who, after adventurous wanderings, reached Palestine aboard the freighter *Astir*), the Rosenbaum school was closed, because the number of the pupils had fallen from over two hundred to thirty-six. "At the end of February eight students [the last] had managed to obtain their secondary diplomas (which were certified by the Senate)." (When, in Jerusalem, I asked Eva Gerson for details, she said: "The Nazis on the examining commission, including Schramm and other bigwigs, were rather impressed by our performance.")

Although I had grown up next door to the martyrdom of the Jews, it was then that I gained the knowledge that enabled me to speak with precision. Through countless affidavits, diary entries, documents, and newspaper reports that I found at Erwin Lichtenstein's, I became aware of the crime that at that time, during my childhood, had slowly been taking on more and more monstrous proportions. Yet I would not have been the right author for a linear chronicle. To expose the many layers of the German trauma I required a present constellation as a counter-theme, for the generations of those who had participated, and of those who knew and kept silent, was not merely inconspicuously present, but was reaching out for new political responsibility as though nothing had happened.

*Dr. Lichtenstein's book appeared in 1973 as *Die Juden der Freien Stadt Danzig unter der Herrschaft des Nationalsozialismus* (Tübingen). —Ed.

In the late 1960s, when the Cold War and the Adenauer era of internal restoration had drawn to a close, there was a possibility, for the first time in the Federal Republic, of a democratic transfer of power. But by letting the parliamentary opposition dwindle to nothing, the government of the Great Coalition, formed of Christian democrats and social democrats, confronted the still-insecure democratic consciousness of the West German people with its first real challenge. On the left, the student protest movement gave rise to an "Extra-parliamentary Opposition"; on the right, the growth of a neofascist party, the NPD, was encouraged by the choice, as chancellor of the Great Coalition, of a man with the political past of Kurt Georg Kiesinger. This seemed to invalidate the arguments of the government parties against the neo-Nazis. As a long-time member of the National Socialist Party, Kiesinger had held important positions under the Third Reich, undeterred to the last by the crimes that were well known to him. His chancellorship was an insult to all those who had resisted Nazism. The political revaluation of his past called into question everything the West Germans, those model students of school democracy, had been teaching one another: political responsibility, return to a liberal system of justice—not merely colorless good behavior, but also shame and grief rooted in knowledge of German crimes that cannot be wished away.

The fact that the Social Democrat and one-time refugee Willy Brandt served as Kiesinger's vice-chancellor and foreign minister could not sweeten the unsavory compromise. Especially the postwar generation, sensitized by the movement of protest against the Vietnam War, rejected the "government of national reconciliation" as lacking in credibility. No amount of street demonstrations or moral appeals could shake the new power cartel, but there was reason to hope that the Bundestag elections, scheduled for the autumn of 1969, might replace Kiesinger and his Great Coalition with a socialist–liberal-democratic coalition headed by Willy Brandt.

I took an active part in the ensuing election campaign. With a group of friends, I helped to organize a Socialist Voters' Drive. For seven months I was on the road, leaving my home in Berlin on Monday and returning at the end of the week. Coming and going, I was confronted with my children's questions: What are you doing? Who are you doing it for? How come Kiesinger was a Nazi? Why did Willy Brandt have to leave Germany when he was young? Exactly what happened to the Jews? And what were you doing then?

For the first time I was confronted by the question: What explanation shall we give our children? It was easy enough to tell them what I had been doing: I was a Hitler Youth, aged seventeen at the end of the war and called up with the last draft, too young to acquire guilt. But when I was asked, "What if you had been older?," it was hard to answer. How could I know for sure what I would have done? The belated anti-Nazism of my generation was never subjected to the danger test. I could not swear that, if I had been six or seven years older, I would not have participated in the great crime. My doubts were such that I was plagued (more and more often as time passed) by night-mares in which I felt myself to be guilty. The dividing line between real and potential action was blurred. My dubious relief at belonging to the "right age group" expressed itself in the stammerings that followed my children's questions in my diary. Interspersed with entries about the election campaign, jottings from the provinces. The present, which was ailing with the past. The demonic idyll. The speed-crazed Today overtaken by Yesterday. German time dislocations. The future postdated. Snail tracks that could be read forward or backward. *From the Diary of a Snail.*

That was to be the title of the book, in which I would tell my children and other children the story of the Danzig Jewish community, mingled with daily items from the present election campaign, shot through with the interaction between melan-cholia and utopia, and roofed over by the principle of Doubt. I wanted to convey to the rising generation the workings of a slow, phase-delayed development of gradual processes which no leap could accelerate, which, on the one hand, have held back social progress and, on the other, first piled up small quantities of guilt that then grew into a monstrous crime: the burden that could no longer be thrown off. I wanted to teach the children that the history which is now taking place in Germany began hundreds of years ago, that these German histories, with the rubble they leave behind them, with their ever new debits of guilt, cannot become obsolete, cannot die away. My unsuccessful attempt to have Heine's Rabbi Abraham escape from fifteenth-century Bacherach to twentieth-century Frankfurt found a sort of counterpart when I suspended chronology, made the 1930s catch up with the 1960s, and denied the leveling power of time.

That the treasure of the Danzig Central Synagogue, the Gieldzinski Collection, is being exhibited in New York today is much more than an artistic event. Many things that cannot be displayed in showcases or on pedestals should at the same time be said and heard. Let us free our time sense from the servitudes of historical correlation. While viewing the collection, let us ponder Heine's medieval Bacherach with its Passover that ended in a pogrom, the Danzig of my childhood with its Jewish community established there for centuries and persecuted out of racist madness, the still-endangered existence of Israel, and the two German states that are sick with the sickness of Heine's century and its ideologies, which are still enslaving humankind. To the question "What are you writing?" my answer was: "A writer, children, is someone who writes against the passage of time."

When my book was finished, all the children had grown older. By then they could have read it, but they didn't want any old stories. Only the present counted. A revolutionary future was being talked into existence. The great leaps that always end in regression were in vogue.

Since then the past has again (once again) caught up with us. Growing children, children who have grown up in the meantime, their several-times-stunned parents, and still-bewildered grandparents sit viewing the *Holocaust* series on their family television screens. Public-opinion institutes have published the first reactions: confessions, horror, rejection, protestations of innocence. Some discover a false historical detail and hasten to condemn the whole series as untrue; some claim to be shattered, as if they had never heard, seen, or read anything of the kind: We didn't know! We were never shown anything like that. Why weren't we told sooner!

Thirty-five years after Auschwitz, the mass media are celebrating their triumph. Nothing counts but mass effect, large numbers. The documents, reportages, analyses that have been available for the past thirty years are meaningless, beside the point; they have failed to reach the masses. Clearly, the written word is too difficult. The catchphrase "mass enlightenment" (the counterpart of "mass destruction") has been used to quash all criticism of a television series that was as successful as it was questionable. And writers, that rare, incurably old-fashioned species, no doubt threatened with extinction, who still expect the individual and the masses to read, are urgently advised to throw their elitist aesthetics overboard, to abandon their subtleties and complexities, and devote themselves to mass enlightenment. In this view the question "What shall we tell our children?" should find its answer (between commercials) on television, where no one else can fail to see and hear it.

I wish to disagree. The success of "popular" enlightenment has never been more than skin-deep. Demonstrably as television series (as shown by public-opinion polls) shatter, touch, or horrify the masses, much as they move them to pity or even shame —and this was the effect of *Holocaust*—they are quite incapable of disclosing the complex "modernity" of genocide and the many-layered responsibilities at the root of it. Basically, Auschwitz was not a manifestation of common human bestiality; it was a repeatable consequence of a network of responsibilities so organized and so subdivided that the individual was conscious of no responsibility at all. The action of every individual who

> This is a delicate pierre — perhaps not beautifully laid

participated or did not participate in the crime was determined, knowingly or unknowingly, by a narrow conception of duty. Only the active agents—Kaduk or Eichmann, for instance—have been condemned, but those who sat dutifully at their desks and all those who suppressed their own powers of speech, who did nothing for but also nothing against, who knew but stood aside—they were not judged, they had not (visibly) soiled their hands.

Up until now the grave guilt of the Catholic and Protestant churches has not been aired. Yet it has been proved that by their passive acceptance they shared in the responsibility for Auschwitz. Attempts of churchmen to justify their actions by adducing reasons of state make it clear that clerically organized Christians took refuge in irresponsibility unless they themselves were endangered, with the exception of certain courageous individuals who acted in disregard of their church's instructions, and of the thus-far-isolated case of the Evangelical Church's "Stuttgart Confession of Guilt." Since Auschwitz, Christian institutions (in Germany, at least) have forfeited their claim to ethical leadership.

The medieval persecutions of the Jews and the deep-rooted Christian hatred of the Jews have been taken over by modern anti-Semitism abetted in recent years by the passive irresponsibility of the churches. Not barbarians or beasts in human form, but cultivated representatives of the religion of human brotherhood allowed the crime to happen: they are more responsible than the criminal in the spotlight, be his name Kaduk or Eichmann.

In Danzig too the bishops of both churches looked on, or stood indifferently aside, when in November 1938 the synagogues in Langfuhr and Zoppot were set on fire and the shrunken Jewish community was terrorized by SA Sturm 96. At that time I was eleven years old and both a Hitler Youth and a practicing Catholic. In the Langfuhr Church of the Sacred Heart, which was ten minutes' walk from the Langfuhr Synagogue, I never, up to the beginning of the war, heard a single prayer in behalf of the persecuted Jews, but I joined in babbling a good many prayers for the victory of the German armies and the health of the Führer, Adolf Hitler. Individual Christians and Christian groups shared the utmost bravery in resisting Nazism, but the cowardice of the Catholic and Protestant churches in Germany made them tacit accomplices.

No television series says a word about that. The many-faceted moral bankruptcy of the Christian West would not lend itself to gripping, shattering, horror-inspiring action. What shall we tell our children? Take a good look at the hypocrites. Distrust their gentle smiles. Fear their blessing.

On Politics

LITERATURE AND REVOLUTION or THE RHAPSODIST'S SNORTING HOBBYHORSE

Address delivered at the Belgrade Writers' Conference, October 17–21, 1969.

Ladies and Gentlemen,

I'll come right out with it: I'm against revolution. I detest the sacrifices that always have to be made in its name. I detest its superhuman goals, its absolute demands, its inhuman intolerance; I fear the mechanism of revolution, which had to invent permanent counterrevolution as an antidote to its efforts. From Kronstadt to Prague, Russia's October Revolution, though a military success, has been a failure in the sense that it restored the traditional structures of political power. Revolutions replace dependence with dependence, coercion with coercion.

In other words, I am at best a tolerated guest among proponents of revolution: I am a revisionist and worse—I am a social democrat.

Since in recent years the people of Western Europe, in mingled terror and fascination, have taken to consuming revolution as a topic of conversation or as material for audiovisual display, and since grandiose revolutionary (and telegenic) gestures have left nothing behind them but intensified reaction (in France, for example), a plethora of secondary revolutionary literature, and a certain influence on men's and women's outer garments, the question arises: can't the most recent revolutionary speculations, as unwarranted as they are unpromising, ultimately be attributed to the dissatisfaction of literary rhapsodists, to whom revolution seems to promise spectacular gestures? In Germany, at all events, it was literary mediocrity that first attempted to get a free ride on the back of the student protest movement. A doctoral thesis might be devoted to the role of literary epigones in proclaiming literary models of revolution. Early in the century it was said that if a revolution were ever to take place in Germany it would be in the field of music. Today—in the late sixties—the revolutionary stance has found a far better subsidized playground: even archconservative newspapers have been running feature articles that foam at the mouth with revolutionary fervor. Literature and revolution, or the rhapsodist's snorting hobbyhorse.

You may have noticed that our topic, apparently so serious, is doing its best to make me abandon all attempts to keep a straight face. For it almost looks as if the grandiloquent heralds of the revolutionary vogue have either failed to read Trotsky's remarks on the subject or as if, against their better judgment, carried away, at least temporarily, by the student protest movement, they had become a demonstration *per absurdum* of the thesis that literature must be the handmaiden of revolution.

I'm determined to spare you and myself any lengthy discussion of the quintessence of this absurdity—namely, socialist realism. We all know that literature today is the most naïve, and therefore the most willing, victim of revolution. The fate of the Russian and Italian futurists shows how quickly a radically antibourgeois literary movement, trusting to revolutionary ideas, can find itself in totalitarian company. In 1924 Trotsky wrote: "After all, didn't Italian Fascism come to power by revolutionary methods, by setting the masses, the mob, the millions, in motion, hardening and arming them? It is no accident and no misunderstanding, but in keeping with scientific laws, that Italian futurism was engulfed in the stream of Fascism." (Later on, Stalinism devoured Russian futurism just as greedily.) Only too often the heralds of revolution have become uncritical apologists for revolutionary terror.

Since August of this year, Paris has been graced with an exhibition in honor of Napoleon, whose two-hundredth birthday Europe is preparing, with mixed feelings, to celebrate. If we consider that, as the Paris exhibition shows, Napoleon never suffered from a lack of literary eulogists, and that Napoleon was a product of the French Revolution, and if we bear in mind that Joseph Stalin must be regarded as a product of the October Revolution—for neither Napoleon nor Stalin dropped from the sky—we are entitled to imagine how colorfully and with what glittering literary encomiums Stalin's two-hundredth birthday will be celebrated when the time comes. And, come to think of it, the inevitable birthdays of the dictators Mussolini and Hitler could be occasions for colossal exhibitions featuring exquisite literary testimonials by writers ranging from Marinetti to Gottfried Benn.

At all times and under all systems, writers have taken advantage of revolutionary occasions to unload their antibourgeois exasperation. To such productive misunderstandings we owe enduringly beautiful poems by Klopstock and Schiller, Yesenin and Mayakovsky. Writers love to transfer purifying storms and showers of metaphors to white paper; but once we try to measure a line of Rimbaud or an Early Expressionist image against reality, the puritanical zeal of the guillotine begins to weigh on us, or we bog down in scholastic discussions of the question: Did Stalin's agrarian reform justify the murder of millions of kulaks?

With blinding clarity the German writer Georg Büchner exposed the deadly mechanisms of revolution: with a few changes in local color, *Danton's Death* might apply to Cuba or China. The truism that revolution devours its children has not yet been refuted. I hear the question coming: Are you implying that the French Revolution or the October Revolution was not necessary? —

We have no way of finding out how and with what consequences the European Enlightenment could have developed without revolution in France, whether the victims of the Revolution might have been spared. We do not know, and we are at a loss to conjecture, how and to what degree the Kerenski government could have democratized tsarist Russia. Those who believe in the logic of revolution will not be convinced by either the English or the Swedish example. But one thing is certain: much as Eisenstein's film *Potemkin* still appeals to us, the price, Stalin and his consequences, seems too high for even the most incorrigible revolutionary rhapsodist.

I come from a country with a tragicomic revolutionary past. From 1848 through 1918 to our most recent Book Fair insurrections, most left-wing revolutions have ended by making themselves ridiculous. We are still paying dearly for what, if you'll forgive me for saying so, may be considered the one successful German revolution: the National Socialist seizure of power in 1933. It is too easy to dispose of Mussolini's March on Rome and Hitler's Thirtieth of January as rightist putsches, as though only left-wing seizures of power were entitled to the name of "revolution."

Though far from equating the aims and motives of leftist and rightist revolutions, I believe that the mechanisms of revolution function independently, regardless of whether the revolution is animated by leftist or by rightist ideologies, of whether the aggressive drives released regard themselves as leftist or rightist. Even the relationship between right-wing literature and right-oriented revolution is not unlike the relationship between left-wing literature and left-oriented revolution. Brecht's hymns to Stalin are in no way superior to Heidegger's kowtowings to National Socialism. If someone were to set up a waxworks museum with prominent literary figures personifying the relationship between literature and revolution, Anna Seghers and Ilya Ehrenburg would have to be grouped with Gottfried Benn and Ezra Pound.

Hérault's demand in Büchner's *Danton's Death*—"It is time for the revolution to stop and the Republic to begin"—is still valid today. But the occupation of Czechoslovakia shows how hard it is being made for the republic to begin, precisely because the revolution can't stop. Which is all the more reason to stop thinking about "Literature and Revolution" and give some consideration to the unspectacular, less inflammatory theme: "Literature and the Republic."

A few weeks ago in my country, a round in the fight for the weal and woe of the republic came to an end. A close victory for the Social Democrats seems to hold out some hope for a German parliamentary democracy whose history has been unstable, full of vicissitudes, and on the whole more unhappy than continuous. It is true that the stimulus word "revolution" was much seen and heard in the period immediately preceding the elections, but when the protest movement ended in violent action and it became clear that the essential conflict was that between the traditional power groups—on the one side the conservatives with their nationalist superstructure, and on the other side the socialist-liberal reformists—the word "revolution" fell into disuse, except perhaps in advertisements for household appliances. Civic common sense showed no inclination to be guided by the verbal radicalism or vulgar anticommunism of the fifties. Medium-range reformist goals, associated with plans for financing, were decisive. Reason managed to extend its base by a hand's breadth.

It was amusing and instructive to observe how this sobering process made itself felt in the political and economic sections of the press, while literature—or, rather, the branch of literature concerned with feature articles—went right on playing revolutionary sandbox games. A few publishers' readers, and, responding to the trend, a few authors embittered for varying reasons, began to avenge themselves on society for its coolness toward revolution by trying systematically to ruin certain reputedly left-wing publishing houses. Nothing surprising about that, for the literary variety of revolution has always been directed primarily against its own camp. In the past three years it has never occurred to the proponents of revolutionary change to dynamite the Hannover Trade Fair; oh no, *their* Bastille has been the Frankfurt Book Fair.

I won't go into details and ask, for instance, whether the storming of a cold buffet is likely to call the attention of the masses to the concentration of power under late capitalism. And the depressing fact that the traditional, formerly right-oriented tendency of students to bug the bourgeoisie for a few carefree years has now slipped into leftist costume, is only one more indication of the pseudorevolutionary character of a fashionable movement, which in the end has revealed only one thing: the internal quarrels of the radical left and its blindness to the alternative—namely, the arduous, long-range attempt to get the republic finally started.

Don't get me wrong: I'm not talking about the student protest movement, which for the most part pressed for reforms and, by radically democratic means, forced public discussion of such matters as long-overdue university reform. I'm talking about the wanton literary abuse of the stimulus word "revolution" and about a group of fast-writing, inflammatory, and immoderately ambitious writers who never weary of celebrating the May 1968 disaster of the French left as a revolutionary achievement and collecting its outpourings in anthologies. And they continue to bask in the illusion that in France the students and intellectuals achieved solidarity with the workers.

During the last election campaign, when overextended wage contracts and failure to revaluate the mark led to spontaneous work stoppages in a number of factories, groups of the radical left, imagining no doubt that the workers were planning something revolutionary, tried to approach the strikers, who patted them good-naturedly on the back and sent them home.

Will this "experience with the masses" teach anyone a lesson? Are the contradictions of daily life in a democracy glaring and sobering enough to deter writers from engaging in do-it-yourself revolutionary activity in their leisure time?

A cynic might say that the literary market will regulate demand. At present, the need for attractively packaged revolutionary literature is more than covered. The most dim-witted high-school student is beginning to realize that the destruction of factories, even if they produce consumer goods, might encounter considerable resistance; that the industrial countries of both the East and the West have to increase their productivity if the already foreseeable catastrophes of the Third World are to be averted; and that it is not up to seminars in German literature to decide whether, when, and for what reasons revolutions should take place in South America.

Let me risk a prediction: if literature wants to be taken seriously, it will have to stop trying to turn the reader on with the stimulus word "revolution." Already there are indications that, especially in Scandinavia (which is ahead of other European countries), more and more writers are beginning to take an interest in the potentialities and limitations of economic development as a factor in peace policy. For the first time "peace studies"—only a few years ago identified with utopian pacifism—are beginning to figure prominently in budgetary debates; if peace, until now an exceptional condition, is to become permanent, it will be necessary to make a scientific study of the peaceful ways of solving conflicts that would normally lead to war.

Will literature be able to get away from the barricades it has been so addicted to thus far? Or will it reverse the road signs and take an interesting, esoteric, and illusory course to romanticism?

"Literature and Revolution"—a gem from Leon Trotsky's literary heritage. Marxist scholastics in naïve discussion with Jesuitical left deviationists. There will always be exclusionists, and they will always applaud themselves, but literature demands realities; for there are more realities than one. I hope to become acquainted with yours, with the Yugoslavian reality; I shall be glad to tell you about mine, the German reality. I start from the assumption that your reality and mine are not mutually exclusive. Our revolutions have already taken place.

ERFURT 1970
AND 1891

Address delivered May 1, 1970, in Baden-Baden.

Citizens of Baden-Baden:

Now that the seventies are beginning, we shall have to give May 1 a new content if it is to become more than a solemn but empty formula. It's not a holiday that should be rented out as a platform for the usual panegyrics.

May 1 isn't suited to the routine promotion of day-to-day trade-union policy, important as that is and much as it concerns us. Today, on this May 1, we shall pursue historical causes, the effects of which are still catching up with us and often enough taking us by surprise.

After twenty years of the German Federal Republic and the German Democratic Republic, after twenty years of the Federation of German Trade Unions and the Free Federation of German Trade Unions, after fifteen years of Bundeswehr and Volksarmee, after the change of government in Bonn,* long-repressed German history and its consequences are overtaking us; we can no longer evade them. Tired of wishful thinking, we are doing something that was long taboo—beginning to recognize reality.

*On October 21, 1969, a coalition of Social Democrats and Free Democrats took office in West Germany, after twenty years of Christian-Democratic governments. —ED.

It's not a pleasant reality. It's painful because it makes us aware of division; and quite a few of us may regret that the new policy has consigned the old harmonious wish-dreams to the archives. For twenty years the word "reunification" and the desire for reunification overshadowed the daily lessons of reality. Reunification was a shibboleth you just had to believe in. And whenever we found an occasion to celebrate—on June 17, May 1, or whatever—we forced ourselves to profess this artificial faith.

But far from moving mountains, faith in reunification hasn't even been able to move the Berlin Wall. Today we are not afraid to come out with what many knew but said only in whispers, what many suspected but for reasons of all-too-understandable orthodoxy didn't even admit to themselves. There will be no reunification, not under our social system and not under Communist auspices. Two German states, more radically different and mutually hostile than anyone could have foreseen, must learn to live side by side and to bear together the burdens of a common history.

How is that to be done? We have so little practice. How are we to live side by side and together? We've seen the pictures from Erfurt.* Willy Brandt and Willi Stoph: two men who were able to take a realistic view of each other. Two politicians, both in precarious positions: the one threatened by Herr Strauss; the other with Honecker, his intraparty rival, breathing down his neck. Honecker and Strauss: ideologically they are worlds apart, but the dogma of the Cold War unites them and makes them hope that what was begun at Erfurt will fail. One often gets the impression that the two Germanys have only one thing in common: absolute negation.

But we've also seen the square between railroad station and hotel. The pictures showed spontaneous joy and cautious hope, but also frenzied, prearranged counteragitation. What we did

*On March 19, 1970, Chancellor Brandt of West Germany and Prime Minister Stoph of East Germany met in the East German city of Erfurt.

not see but have learned since then, is that a few citizens of the German Democratic Republic have got into trouble for merely reacting spontaneously—because Communism doesn't tolerate spontaneity and because the inhuman logic of Communist dogma demands hardness even in situations where an admission of weakness would bring the responsible politicians of the GDR sympathy.

And yet only pleasant things happened in Erfurt. We saw that a statesman, who only a short time ago was defamed in both German states, enjoys the confidence of our neighboring compatriots. When Willy Brandt came to the window, it was not to receive ovations but to give thanks and ask forbearance for his difficult task.

He was understood. But did we understand the picture showing the Chancellor of the Federal Republic in the former Buchenwald concentration camp? Laying a wreath. Just the usual gesture? Or was it more? In the Buchenwald concentration camp German Communists and Social Democrats were murdered by German National Socialists. Wherever we set foot, we run into harsh reminders of the past. Hardly a patch of ground without its pitfalls, hardly a word without a double meaning.

Erfurt too has more than one meaning. It means something else besides March 19, 1970. In the over a hundred years of the history of German Social Democracy and the German trade-union movement, the history of the city of Erfurt carries a more oppressive weight than many German Social Democrats and trade unionists care to admit.

On this May 1 it should be a useful pleasure for you and for me to look back and recall what else Erfurt means.

In 1891, a year after the repeal of Bismarck's Antisocialist Laws, the Social Democratic Party of Germany held a party congress in Erfurt. At that momentous party congress the Erfurt Program was promulgated. This party program gave rise to an intraparty conflict that lasted a long time, was soon to shape the working-class movement throughout Europe, and is still going on under scarcely different conditions. I am speaking of the revisionism conflict and its consequences, of a conflict that weakened the Socialist working-class movement for years, later split it completely, and culminated in deadly hostility. Erfurt 1891 and Erfurt 1970. History doesn't repeat itself, but it has the memory of an elephant. Let us look back.

Up to the time of the Erfurt party congress, German Social Democracy was influenced more by Lassalle's theories than by Marx and Engels. In 1869, when the Social Democrats of Eisenach, under Bebel and the Lasalleans, founded the Social Democratic Labor Party in Gotha, Marx and Engels were skeptical. The two rigorous theorists in their London exile were far removed from the practical work of the German Social Democrats. Despite mutual admiration, the two wings of the party were separated by increasing misunderstanding. Even August Bebel's emancipatory work *Women and Socialism* was influenced more by the French utopian socialist Charles Fourier than by Marx and Engels.

The hitherto prevailing program, promulgated at the party congress in Gotha, had been violently criticized by Marx at the time; after that, its author, Wilhelm Liebknecht, could no longer be regarded as the party's leading theoretician.

During the twelve years of persecution, while the Antisocialist Laws were in force, all Socialist newspapers and periodicals had been suppressed. There was no available organ in which to develop the theories of Ferdinand Lassalle and to purge them of their Prussian, state-socialist bias. The Social Democratic Party emerged from the years of persecution strong in membership and new hopes, but in a spiritual and theoretical vacuum.

The only Social-Democratic theoreticians to maintain close contact with Friedrich Engels during the eighties were Karl Kautsky and Eduard Bernstein. With Engels's support and the authority of August Bebel, they drafted the Erfurt Program. A few years after the death of Karl Marx, the Marxist scientific approach and dogmatism found their way into the programmatic foundations of the German working-class movement. The Erfurt Program falls into two parts: the theoretical part can be attributed to Kautsky, the practical part to Bernstein. This duality between revolutionary aims and the practical striving for reform marks the beginning of the party's split into revolutionaries and reformists. Kautsky and Bernstein, the fathers of the Erfurt Program, are also the fathers of the conflict, which is still in progress. It was certainly not their intention to split the party; it was the contradictions in Marxism, already present in Marx himself, that stood in the way of a dialectical synthesis between theory and practice.

One almost gets the impression that the Erfurt Program divided the Socialist week into a revolutionary Sunday and six busy, reformist working days. And yet the revolutionary aims of the Kautsky-Bebel wing were purely theoretical. The reformist politicians Bernstein and Vollmar ridiculed the revolutionary Sunday speeches of certain Social Democrats, who on weekdays went soberly and matter-of-factly about their reformist tasks.

Here are the contradictions in the Erfurt Program.

Kautsky (and with him Bebel) set an ultimate goal: the transformation of capitalist property—especially private ownership of the means of production—into socialized property. Both men built on the Marxist theory of the imminent collapse and demise of capitalism and, with it, of bourgeois society. Their program, in theory at least, amounted to a radical declaration of war on the existing social order; it precludes participation in parliaments, even in the role of an opposition.

In contrast to this was the practical, working program: Bernstein and Georg von Vollmar, who collaborated with the program commission, called for specific improvements in the social situation of workers and women. They emphasized the importance of legislation, recognized the parliament as a democratic institution where the desired reforms could be achieved, and set Social-Democratic goals that even at the time entered into the sphere of practical politics, though they were not attained until decades later; women's suffrage, for instance, and the abolition of the death penalty.

The practical part of the program aims at developing a democracy based partly on direct popular vote, partly on representation; it stresses the "self-administration of the people in Reich, state, province, and community" and the "election of officials by the people."

Today we may wonder why the tragicomical contradictions in the Erfurt Program created such long-lasting confusion. Quite aside from Marx's catastrophe theory, predicating the imminent demise of capitalism, the long period of repression had led even moderate Social Democrats to hope for liberation through revolution. The correspondence between August Bebel and Friedrich Engels shows how every crisis of the capitalist economy led these ordinarily sober-minded thinkers to engage in wild speculation. They set their hopes in the pauperization of the toiling masses, while in their day-to-day reformist efforts they were doing their best to remedy this same pauperization. Revolution was taken as a sacred article of faith, but it was more urgent to relieve the misery of the working class. During twelve years of persecution, while the Antisocialist Laws were in force, August Bebel was able to bridge this contradiction, of which he himself, with his faith in revolution and his practical work as a great parliamentarian, was a part and an expression.

By and large it can be said that the theoretical section of the Erfurt Program rejects a form of society that the practical section of the same program takes for granted but tries to improve along democratic lines and to consolidate by means of social reforms.

Nearly a century later, there cannot be much point in being a know-it-all and putting the blame on a betrayal of revolutionary ideas or an unscientific lack of realism. It is hard for us to appraise the harm done by the Antisocialist Laws or to appreciate the greatness of August Bebel's achievement in carrying the impoverished and disorganized working-class movement through twelve years of famine. At that time the Erfurt Program met with the approval of the whole party; it was accepted almost unanimously. After years of persecution the Socialists were glad to have ground under their feet again.

Today we can see that theory and practice were incompatible —indeed, mutually exclusive; that the program was such as to split the working-class movement not only in Germany but, as it would turn out, in all of Europe. For the German Social Democratic Party was taken as a model throughout Europe, imitated in its strength and in its weakness.

Only a few years later the practical politicians tried to bridge the disastrous gap between the practical section of the program and its utopian, more or less unscientific theoretical section, by persuading the following party congresses to revise the program; since then they have been termed "revisionists," a political epithet that has never lost its pejorative connotation. After the Soviet occupation of Czechoslovakia, Alexander Dubček and Ota Sik, the theoreticians of Czechoslovakian reformed Communism, were anathematized as "revisionists."

If we search history for comparisons, we find a similar dogmatic rigidity in the heresy trials of the Middle Ages. Giordano Bruno, the Albigenses, the Hussites, and the Lutherans were all regarded as revisionists by dogmatic Catholics, and made to pay for it.

Eduard Bernstein, the most eminent revisionist of his day, was defeated by the verbal-revolutionary wing of his party. We have begun only recently to realize how far in advance of his time Bernstein was with his foresight and soberly scientific attitude. His early opposition to the "dictatorship of the proletariat" as an ultimate goal made him, when Lenin chose that course, one of the first critics of Communist totalitarianism. Bernstein was the first Socialist to dare to oppose the superstitious Marxist belief in the impending collapse of bourgeois capitalist society. He warned against raising wishful thinking to the level of a theory. He proved that the capitalist economy has "powers of adaptation" and is not governed by eternal and immutable Marxist laws. And yet, though Bernstein's analysis was confirmed time and time again, wishful thinking and dogmatic superstition continued to dominate the Socialist parties.

Let me cite one example from recent times. Whenever the New Left refers to capitalism as "late capitalism," it supports such wishful thinking by implying, without proof, that capitalism is in a late—that is, final—phase.

Yet we could learn from history that capitalism is as old or as young as socialism, that they condition and influence each other; indeed, that the expropriation of private capital under the dictatorship of the proletariat has led, not to the end of capitalism, but to a new form of repression established by Lenin —namely, socialist state capitalism. When Willy Brandt and Willi Stoph, the Social Democrat and the Communist, met in Erfurt, they represented not only the historical split in Socialism and the nation, but also the social orders of private capitalism and state capitalism; more than seventy years ago, Eduard Bernstein perceived the adaptability of capitalism; it is not wedded to private ownership.

But before I go back to Erfurt 1970, I'd like to say a word more about Erfurt 1891. It's rewarding to look into the cause of Socialist self-destruction and the beginnings of the modern Social-Democratic reform policy. For, disastrously as the Erfurt Program weakened and finally split the European working-class movement, the conflicts that followed it added enduringly to the self-confidence of those workers who had organized in their shops and factories. The beginnings of revisionism went hand in hand with an increase in the political power of the unions. The members of the cooperative and trade-union movements, who were confronted each day with the problems of practical politics, were the first to realize how necessary it was to revise the unrealistic theories of the Erfurt Program.

Bernstein's idea that the cooperatives help to operate and supervise the means of production may be regarded as the first draft of the worker-participation schemes that are under discussion today. And the Godesberg Program* may be regarded as a late victory for revisionist reform policy. But that too is already in need of revision, if only because all reform policy is in permanent need of revision.

Worker participation, insofar as it is conceived as an effective means of supervision, might be the democratic alternative to the traditional private capitalism of our social order and the traditional state capitalism of the Communist social order. It will be attainable only as a global form extending to every sphere of society—school and university, job site, and courthouse. Being a reformist task, it must take an evolutionary course.

There would be no point in following the example of the Erfurt Program and formulating a revolutionary theory as a guideline for worker participation. A glance back at history should teach us that a party program whose theoretical section proceeds by revolutionary leaps and bounds while its practical section prescribes slow reforms, will at best foster a split consciousness. There is no such thing as a jumping snail.

But, we might ask, now that the working-class movement is split, is there no hope of a reconciliation between revolutionaries and reformists, between Communists and Social Democrats? Might the meeting between Willy Brandt and Willi Stoph not mark a first step in this direction?

If we look closely, we see that the very conflicts that found their expression in the Erfurt Program almost eighty years ago were present as potential dynamite in Erfurt 1970. The undogmatic road to socialism has too long been defamed as revisionism. The costs and sacrifices occasioned by the revolutionary wing of the European working-class movement have been too great. The loss of basic democratic rights in the Communist countries cannot be compensated by the transformation of private capitalism into state capitalism—in other words,

*The Godesberg Program was formally adopted by the German Social Democratic Party at a conference in the city of Bad Godesberg, November 11–13, 1959. —ED.

by the substitution of a new form of oppression for an old one.

Social Democracy and Communism can probably coexist; they can't mix. Those who dream of reunification are in for a rude awakening. People who build on such hopes have learned nothing from history. The Communists still regard Social Democracy as the archenemy. You have only to look at Ulbricht's writings; to his mind revisionism, reformism, and Social Democracy are equally heretical, and equally earmarked for persecution.

Nor, however, has the revisionist controversy ended in the West. No one who has kept abreast of the discussions among students in the last three years can fail to see that the revolutionary demands of a minority cannot be reconciled with the reformist aims of a majority. What anachronistic vehemence has been wasted on the question of whether and under what circumstances the use of violence is permissible. How rhetorically the word "revolution" has been bandied about, and how nimbly the fashions in revolutionary attitudes have changed. How bitterly the various groups within the revolutionary wing have wrangled with one another, and what accusations these revolutionaries, deaf to the lessons of history, have exchanged.

But the internal struggles within the Socialist Student League were merely a reflection of the increasing tensions within the world Communist movement. The same Soviet Union that first combated Yugoslavian Titoism and then Czechoslovakian democratic socialism as revisionism is now accused of the same heresy by the People's Republic of China.

I doubt if anyone today stops to think what the word "revisionism" really means and how necessary it is to submit existing schemas to permanent revision. The now classical epithet has been taken over unexamined; and yet, in the midst of so much dogmatic rigidity, there is good reason to regard the accusation "revisionist" as an honor.

I therefore take May 1, 1970, as an occasion to call the much-reviled Eduard Bernstein a farsighted and important social democrat.

Such reminders are necessary. The Socialist Party of Germany and the Federation of German Trade Unions have been much too negligent and forgetful about their own past. Too many young Social Democrats are embarrassed to mention Eduard Bernstein's name, though as revisionists they are combating the sclerosis of their own party. The poison of defamation has been effective down to our day.

Eduard Bernstein was born in Berlin in 1850. He was the seventh child of a locomotive engineer. At the age of twenty-two, he joined the Social Democratic Labor Party, which had then been in existence for three years. Employed as a bank clerk, he was obliged to leave Germany at the time of the Antisocialist Laws. For seven years he was editor of the Zurich periodical *Socialdemokrat*. After that he lived in London, in close contact with Friedrich Engels, whose testamentary executor he became in 1895. Fortunately for German social democracy, Bernstein's long stay in England shaped his attitude toward parliamentary democracy. After the Erfurt Party Congress, he began to criticize the party's official Marxist orthodoxy, and to contrast it with the reform policy that was everywhere in force. In his main work, *Evolutionary Socialism*, he sums up his revisionist ideas. During the First World War he voted against the war credits and joined the USPD (Independent Social Democratic Party) for a time. Violently attacked and slandered, Bernstein worked up to the time of his death in 1932, laying the foundations of a modern, undogmatic social democracy. If today for the first time in my generation the Social Democratic Party has won government responsibility, this success can be attributed in large part to Eduard Bernstein's spadework.

Anyone wishing to gain a complete understanding of Erfurt 1970, of the meeting between the social-democratic Chancellor Willy Brandt and the communist Prime Minister Willy Stoph, will have to take cognizance of Erfurt 1891—that is, of the Erfurt

Program and its consequences. Historic events cannot be understood in isolation. The split in the German working-class movement and the split in the German nation are present realities, whose causes have too long been ignored.

History offers us no consolation. It has dealt harsh lessons. For the most part, it reads absurdly. True, it progresses, but progress is not its end result. History has no end; we are in and not outside history.

I have spoken about a very recent historical event: Erfurt 1970. There can be no better day than May 1 on which to recall what else Erfurt means.

WRITERS AND
THE TRADE UNIONS

Address delivered November 20, 1970, at the first Writers'
Conference of the Writers' Association in Stuttgart.

Fellow workers:

This form of address points to the fact that writers and trade
unionists have at least one thing in common—they both invoke
the concept of brotherhood. Something of the old guild spirit
persists and is applied with unremitting rigor. One rebukes
conduct unbecoming to a fellow worker.

Writers and trade unionists, the small Writers' Association of
individualists and that mass organization the Federation of German Trade Unions view each other with mixed feelings. They
respect each other at a distance and distrust each other at close
quarters.

A hundred and twenty years ago, when the working-class
movement and the unions were in their beginnings, there was
more give and take between writers and proletarian organiza-
tions. Not content with their places in the house of literature,
Heine, Freiligrath, and Herwegh played an active part in the
history of socialism, and even where they failed, they were in
the forefront of a development that, though permanently ham-
pered by schism, may be termed successful. But by the middle
of the past century, when Karl Marx was editor-in-chief of the
Neue Rheinische Zeitung, few writers thought of themselves as

members of the working class. Most identified with the bourgeoisie.

And seventy years later, Lenin's opinion of Zurich Dadaism and Trotsky's appraisal of Russian and Italian futurism suggest that the attempts of a few writers to make a radical break with their bourgeois ties provoked skeptical or hostile reactions in the revolutionary leaders of the proletariat. And the fact that the Italian variant of literary futurism easily found its way into the mainstream of Fascism lends weight to the skepticism of Lenin and Trotsky.

Dependent as workers are on their unions, they have often had good reason to regard writers as hard to organize, arrogantly elitist, and, where allied with state communism, corrupt. Noncommittal good intentions, an occasional impulse to send telegrams of solidarity, a sentimental view of the workers, wrapped in coldly scientific phraseology, are indications of the traditionally flawed and contradictory relationship between writers and trade unionists. Conversely, the unions have developed a deep-seated and, I can only say, irrational distrust of intellectuals. Feelings of inferiority are compensated by aggressive blue-collarism. Fear of too-rigid organization has its counterpart in fear of irresponsible ideas, fancy language, know-it-all-ness.

Thus far, most writers and theoreticians of the bourgeois left have been unable to pass this threshold, to dissociate themselves from the enlightened bourgeoisie and regard themselves as persons dependent on wages, as workers requiring the protection of the unions. Recently there has been talk of one more attempt. It is beginning to dawn on both parties that cooperation between workers and unions might at least be worth considering.

Once bitten, twice shy: talking together and, as I've often observed, jestingly addressing one another as fellow workers marks the beginning of an experiment whose consequences it may take some time to appraise.

In the last twenty years, writers have been asked a good many questions that cast doubt on their right to exist. Is there a basic incompatibility between intellect and power? Has it been permissible to write since Auschwitz? Is it possible to write the truth? Useful questions. The kind of questions that are asked on the late-night show. Questions and answers that have been published and gathered into anthologies.

Now we are being called into question in a different way. Our first negotiations with the Federation of German Trade Unions show how very questionable we are. Are we capable of working for scale wages? Are we *willing* to work for scale wages? If so, are we willing to go on strike? Are we, as writers, prepared to recognize the prevailing wage and arbitration laws? And can we name an employers' organization that might be able and willing to negotiate a wage agreement with us? If we are neither employers nor employees, what are we?

When asked, the unions, taking a cool and not unfriendly view, reply that we are employeelike individuals, comparable to home workers. And since the federal labor court has recognized the possibility of a wage scale for home work, there is some chance that we too will be favored with this blessing. It will not be difficult for writers to claim the right to organize on the strength of Article 9, Paragraph 3, of the constitution, which assures all persons, regardless of their occupation, of the right to form associations with a view to obtaining and securing satisfactory conditions of employment and remuneration. Thus, if we so decide, we shall within the foreseeable future be eligible as associated writers for membership either in the Artists' Union or the Printers' and Paper Workers' Union, and thus be in a position to conclude wage agreements.

But do we want to be organized? Are writers capable of the minimum of solidarity that is the obvious *sine qua non* of trade unionism? Won't writers, incorrigible loners that they are, take fright when a mass organization offers them the sweaty smell of solidarity? Won't our bourgeois special interests have the last word? Are we the way we talk? Are we as daring in action as we often are in our writing? Can we be taken seriously when, writing from a safe distance, we refer to on-the-job conditions —I'm speaking of blast furnaces and assembly lines—as exploitation? Are we willing to give up this safe and well-rehearsed distance if only experimentally and to become dependent on people who are themselves in a state of dependency?

These questions are no joke. Not we but the unions will be incurring the greater risk, if they admit us to their ranks. After short-winded enthusiasm, writers have only too often taken refuge in noncommittal attitudes. Eloquent arrogance and a pedantic harping on details have always offered hospitable shelter to those wishing to withdraw discreetly from loudly proclaimed social commitments.

Though for social and economic reasons I strongly favor the admission of writers to the Printers' and Paper Workers' Union, the unions must explicitly be warned against us. We must realize that workers cannot reasonably be expected to accept writers in their unions if we mean to be mere beneficiaries.

So, something is expected of us in return? And I see the suspicion arising: could it be something unseemly—some sort of hack writing, adulatory support, for instance?

And what's to prevent the unions from resuscitating their superannuated suspicions: "They're just putting on airs, they're only interested in themselves, they'll only make trouble"?

Let me try to outline a realistic offer, though I'm well aware that it can expect no more than a hesitant interest on either side.

If writers want to organize into unions, what do they, what do we bring with us?

I say it is our talents, our ability to write, our precision, our love of storytelling, our memories trained to accuracy. Further: our necessary and therefore inevitable inclination to esotericism, the pleasure we take in criticism, our love of the *mot juste*, our gift for taking a naïve attitude toward meaningless bustle; our obstinate restlessness, our existential bond with paper and the printed word.

Where might writers be used effectively? Wherever in the trade-union press inarticulateness pads out lines, where hopeless sclerosis prevents the unions from addressing the public effectively. Wherever pent-up rage on the job cries out for precise expression.

Where can writers help? Wherever this knowledge and ability are needed: in the trade-union schools, to give concrete meaning to the still-abstruse concept of worker participation. They can help enormously by presenting the dozens of isolated reforms in context and picturing them in all their epic breadth. From my own experiences I know how helpful it can be when writers, without in any way sacrificing their convictions or style, speak out on May 1, instead of making gratuitously festive remarks.

Is that too much? Is it too little? Now that Gustav Heinemann is President of our Republic and Willy Brandt, who resisted National Socialism, Chancellor, we writers are for the first time finding an opportunity to work our way out of the roles foisted upon us by tradition and education; and to act as a force for change, not outside but within society.

If the term "organized writer" is not to carry a forbidding overtone, we must be something more than a special-interest group. For just as the unions are at last beginning to see themselves as a force extending beyond wage scales to education and Third World development, so writers have recently begun to take an interest in conflicts that are no longer predominantly products of the war and of the postwar period.

In the complex day-to-day life of a democracy, peace, that still-unexplored territory, confronts us with unaccustomed tasks. No more decisive battles fraught with history, no more Götterdämmerung or invocations of ultimate goals, no *Weltgeist* on horseback. Instead, such problems as phase displacement, the new irrationality of technological mysticism, aggressions spawned by the mass media, terrorism, productivity, the parallel increase of pollution and prosperity are beginning to find their authors.

Who will write about the slow death of Lake Constance? About the degradation and defense of the environment, the crisis in the educational system of a society dedicated to frenetic achievement, about the surfeit that comes of glut? What writers will give these issues form and content while steering clear of the current jargon and ready-made formulas? And what readers, what new readers will they attract? What literature will free the concept of property from its twofold puritanical servitude and give it elbow room in an area between Western private capitalism and communist state capitalism?

As long as the Federal Republic has existed, Article 14 of the constitution has provided, "Property confers an obligation." We know how cleverly our rulers have passed this injunction by. We know the tricks with which they have exempted large property owners from this obligation. Intellectual property has kept different company. The attitude of writers toward property offers the Chancellor and the government a model of public-spirited conduct. There is no reason why landed property and large fortunes should be inherited from generation to generation when intellectual property is, quite properly, relegated to the public domain after a suitable time lapse and devoted to the welfare of the public at large.

Because copyright law is handled as a social obligation, I call it the only law that today complies with the injunction "Property confers an obligation." I can think of no better starting point for the conversations soon to be held between the writers and the unions.

A WARNING AGAINST
THE FORCE OF HABIT

Address delivered in March 1972 in Athens.

Ladies and Gentlemen:

The Society for the Study of Greek Problems has invited me, as a writer and a social democrat, to address you. I thank you for the invitation. Let me start by hinting at what I would like to talk about but can't, what I might talk about but don't wish to, what I am obliged to pass over in silence, and will with your consent.

When I speak here of democracy, every Greek democrat knows which democracy is meant, how it was lost, who made it a laughingstock before it was lost, and what the loss of democratic rights means.

You know the history of your country. You don't need a guest speaker to tell you how dictatorship has succeeded in perpetuating itself since 1936, what third-rate comedians are talented enough to play the role of Metaxas today,* and why, whenever history repeats itself, its tragedies are played as farce.

I needn't go into the economic background because all the special-interest groups that opposed democracy in Greece in the

---

*Ioannis Metaxas (1871–1941), dictator of Greece from 1936 as prime minister, foreign minister, and acting war minister; successfully directed Greek resistance after the Italian attack of October 1940. —ED.

thirties and sixties are known to you. Nor is it up to me to judge the democratic parties whose opportunism or ideological blindness undermined the credibility of democracy and were in part responsible for its downfall. It would be equally pointless for me to name names and military ranks, especially since such names and ranks are interchangeable and are mere window dressing for a will that is dangerously latent throughout Europe, the will to bring back totalitarianism. The example of Greece has helped to mold it.

Nor do I wish to take refuge in parables, let alone drape myself in historical costume. You won't hear anything about Hölderlin and the enthusiasm of romantic youth for Greece, or about Lord Byron, and there won't be any references to Iphigenia and her soulful yearning for Greece. Just this: The Greeks and the Germans have both had an unhappy, often interrupted relationship with democracy, not, like the English, a steadily growing one. For that reason it would ill become a German to give you lessons in democracy, especially since democracy, that still-inspiring concept, had its origin in Greece. Here it was founded, here it perished, and here it was dug up again. Here was shown what power can emanate from the rule of the people. And here was shown for all to see what an emptily pompous figure total state power cuts when the people are disenfranchised and deprived of their democratic rights.

Greece is Europe. When freedom languishes in Greece, Europe is the poorer. Because you have been deprived of your democratic rights, ours are threatened. Democracy has gained acceptance not in its birthplace but elsewhere; now its grateful student comes to you with empty hands and is at a loss for words.

Now that I've hinted at what must not be said, let me introduce myself. Born in 1927 in Danzig on the Baltic Sea, I was six in 1933, twelve in 1939. In May 1945 I was seventeen, too young to participate in the crimes of National Socialism, but old enough to have been shaped by their consequences. Innocent through no fault of my own, perhaps only accidentally without guilt, I have a low opinion of belated antifascism. But I honor the resistance that knows the risks and takes them.

During the first postwar years I accustomed myself slowly and at first reluctantly to a social form that was then unknown to me, which is called democracy and which—according to the constitution—guarantees basic democratic rights. With curiosity I tested my possibilities, gained my first understanding of freedom in art, and was frightened when I first became aware of society and my dependence on it.

In 1949, when for the first time elections were held in two German states, only the Federal Republic was able to come out for free elections and a secret ballot, while in the German Democratic Republic the National Socialist practice of manipulated elections was perpetuated under Communist auspices. I chose evolutionary democratic socialism, though I did not become a member of the Social Democratic Party. It was not in revolutionary upheaval but in slow reform that I saw a possibility of bringing about change as understood by the European Enlightenment.

It may be that as a writer I derived my ideas from the downfall of the Weimar Republic. The entire blame cannot be attributed to the National Socialists' will to power, the opportunism of the German Nationalists, the intolerance of the Communists, and the weakness of the democratic parties. It must also be said that the majority of German writers made no attempt to defend the Republic, while not a few of them deliberately held it up to ridicule.

Here there was a lesson to be learned. Only the Social Democratic Party, even where it has been weak to the point of impotence, can boast constant democratic behavior. It helped me to discover the concept of democracy, which with its sober realism immunized me against flights of enthusiasm. To put it succinctly, a democracy without social justice can be a democracy in name alone; as history shows, a socialism without basic democratic rights leads to one-party dictatorship. Accused of heresy by the Communists, slandered by the conservatives in their alliance with rightist reaction, wedged between the ideological blocs, democratic socialism must nevertheless prove an active force by fighting for its program of social reform and for a parliamentary majority. In this struggle, which has been going on for just a hundred years, we won a close, much-too-close, victory in 1969. Now it will be seen whether democracy and socialism presuppose and do not exclude each other, whether they further or impede each other, whether or not they are interdependent.

The constitution of the German Federal Republic, with its promise of social justice, is the best constitution that has ever been promulgated in Germany, but the political reality does not correspond sufficiently to the constitutional norm. Social justice has thus far remained a promise, the German educational system favors the children of the privileged, the fiscal system favors the wealthy, and German society, with its vulgar materialism and accent on achievement, fails to give children and the elderly, the handicapped and the unsuccessful adequate social protection. Thus it is no wonder that Article 14 of the constitution, with its explicit yet vague sentences—"Property confers obligations. Its use should at the same time benefit the community at large"—has today become a choice instrument of Social-Democratic reform policy.

In the early sixties I started doing day-to-day political work. The presumptuous elitist notion that writers are the conscience of the nation and should rise above the practical realities of politics has always gone against my grain. I traveled from province to province and tried to help the Social Democrats in their election campaign. I was taking a risk, because politics is greedy. The man who's talking to you is a writer and a citizen. Someone who has stopped asking himself: Should I or shouldn't I? Someone who couldn't be satisfied with sitting at his writing desk, but at the same time someone to whom resignation is no stranger and who knows the meaning of failure.

I know all the arguments against dual activity: A writer should keep his distance. Day-to-day politics with its insipid jargon is ruinous to literary style. And, above all, intellect and power are incompatible.

Here's my answer. A writer must face up to the test of reality, including political reality; and that can't be done if he keeps his distance. A literary style cultivated like a hot-house plant may show a certain artificial purity, but it won't be really pure. And as for the old cliché—intellect versus power—I call it a fiction, because power can be intelligent and intelligence can be powerful; and often enough intelligence sells itself to power, and just as often intelligent politics has foundered.

My years of apprenticeship in democracy ran parallel to a worldwide development that detracted from democracy and shook its self-confidence. The West's response to the dogmatic Stalinism of the fifties was to develop, not a strong, pluralistic social democracy as an alternative, but a dogmatic anticommunism. From then on the whole world was seen in black and white. From then on both sides decried the political adversary as an enemy. From then on democratic socialists were blindly suspected of subservience to Moscow—or persecuted and condemned to death or imprisonment as agents of capitalism.

Panic fear of Communism destroyed the Western democracies' awareness of their strength. Lack of self-confidence led them to form anticommunist alliances with rightist dictatorships, regardless of the cost. At first NATO, conceived as a counterforce to the Warsaw Pact, represented itself as a military alliance for the defense of the Western democracies. But soon political reality made a mockery of such intentions. Portugal isn't the only member of NATO to deny its citizens democratic rights.*

Having lost all meaning, the democratic phraseology of the first NATO years was gradually smothered in security jargon

---

*This was written in 1972. In 1974 Caetano, who in 1968 had replaced the ailing Dr. Salazar as dictator of Portugal, was overthrown. Since then Portugal has been governed as a democracy. —Ed.

and at length buried altogether; yet today even military experts can scarcely deny that the NATO members Portugal, Greece, and Turkey are rather shaky pillars of security.

Thus the ideological anticommunism of the Western democracies proved to be a weakness. Its so-called policy of strength has been counterproductive. For two decades the Western democracies—including the German Federal Republic—have failed to reform themselves in the direction of social democracy. This period seems to be coming to an end, even though the peace policy initiated by Chancellor Willy Brandt in the name of innumerable democrats is still vulnerable.

Suppose we draw up a comparative balance sheet. Western private capitalism and Eastern state capitalism, both endangered yet both virtually frozen in their confrontational stance. Both blocs are groaning under the weight of mounting military expenditure and their resulting inability to finance needed internal reforms. Reduced to stereotypes, they take refuge time and time again—after moments of insecurity—in black-and-white Cold War phraseology. Both blocs are indeed endangered, but because they are endangered, they are prepared to take ruthless action.

In the late sixties, for example, comparable events occurred in the two blocs. Since April 21, 1967, the NATO member Greece has not been a democracy; on August 21, 1968, Czechoslovakia, a member of the Warsaw Pact, was occupied by the armies of five other Warsaw Pact states.

In both cases the protagonists of the bloc systems must be held responsible. Without the consent—or, indeed, the support —of the United States, basic democratic rights could not have been abolished in Greece; without the imperial will of the Soviet Union the Czechoslovakian attempt to create a human— and that still means a democratic—socialism would not have been crushed. The pretexts for these two illegal and arbitrary acts of terror are comparable. In Greece, it was allegedly necessary to prevent a Communist takeover; in Czechoslovakia an alleged capitalist-imperialist putsch had to be forestalled. Talk of the internal enemy is a technocrat's way of saying: Our vital interests are threatened.

Greece and Czechoslovakia were treated not as countries where human beings were trying to live their lives in freedom, but (abstractly and therefore inhumanly) as mere security factors. For the sake of allegedly endangered security, one country was robbed of its democratic system of government, and another occupied and deprived of its right of self-determination.

Of course the brutality of both actions had to be covered over with ideological whitewash. In one case the betrayers of basic democratic rights represented themselves as guardians of law and order; in the other, the occupying powers claimed to be defending the people from ideological contamination and counterrevolutionary machinations. Since Stalin and Hitler, the language of political crime, whether committed by left or by right totalitarianism, has become international and intelligible to all. It is a jargon characterized by interchangeable phrases—"decisive action," "mopping up," "re-education."

The holders of state power often affect the solicitous tone of a benevolent paterfamilias. What the American government calls "pacification" in Vietnam, the Soviet forces of occupation call "normalization." And the normalizers and apostles of napalm-pacification have already fallen victim to their own propaganda. They actually believe they are pacifying and normalizing where they are only spreading terror—just as the medieval crusaders thought they were disseminating a religion of charity while they were spreading methodical terror.

Centuries ago, euphemistic language helped, as it does today, to make political crimes look "normal" after a certain lapse of time. A calculation that has worked time and time again. For those who planned and executed attacks on basic democratic rights were sure, when maturing their designs, that time was on their side. After the first wave of indignation, after the first loud protests, the world would "get used to it."

Let's face it: the political criminals of yesterday have regained their respectability, because people have got used to their crimes.

One doesn't have to look far for an example. Three years after Hitler's seizure of power, a number of kings and prime ministers, honorable men and impeccable democrats, gathered in Berlin. Along with the Olympic games of 1936 in Berlin, they celebrated, whether that was their intention or not, the respectability of Hitler and his National Socialist dictatorship. It didn't seem to trouble them that simultaneously with the Olympic contests people were being tortured and murdered in concentration camps nearby. The cheers that greeted Olympic records and youthful achievements drowned out ugly background noises. Once people had got used to the terror that by then was everyday practice, they began to hobnob with its perpetrators.

Apparently the cynicism of political power knows no bounds. The technological age broadcasts it unvarnished. Smiling urbanely, it displays itself on television screens.

Here again there's no need to look far for an example.

While Richard Nixon, President of the United States, and Chou En-lai, Premier of the People's Republic of China, were politely toasting each other, while the Chinese ballet was executing revolutionary leaps before an appreciative public, while Mrs. Nixon was finding Chinese schoolchildren cute and showering them, free of charge, with greetings from America, North Vietnam was being subjected to daily pattern bombing, women and children were dying.

You, ladies and gentlemen, have been made painfully aware of the cynicism of political power. Not only the Western democracies, but the Communist people's republics as well are doing their best, openly or secretly—with occasional signs of embarrassment—to maintain good commercial relationships, at the very least, with the government of your country. Statesmen from East and West are beginning to arrive here. They all claim to be ideologically neutral. Without batting an eyelash, they speak of peaceful coexistence. They supply armaments and with them the pious justification that said armaments are unsuited to civil war and therefore—believe it or not—not directed against the people. I don't want to give you any false hopes. One who has learned that moral appeals are most helpful to those who have formulated them neatly, one who is unable to proclaim a shining new faith, can offer only skepticism.

But I can say this much: justice can be perverted, but even perverted, it remains recognizable. It has been possible to frustrate democratic socialism by violence, but by virtue of the very violence imprinted on it, it leaves its impression on the minds of men: unmistakably. Yes; the mighty may sit secure in their bastions, but they cannot leave them without fear. The power of the state is omnipresent, but since it must be omnipresent, it is also overextended.

Not long ago I had a dream. I saw bloated state power strutting on both sides; I saw the disenfranchised people looking on. I saw bloated state power trying to look dignified, and I saw that its efforts made it more and more ridiculous. And when state power realized that its efforts to look dignified made it more and more ridiculous, it went red in the face with anger, and this new exertion made it more ridiculous than ever. And because the disenfranchised people saw its grotesqueness steadily expanding, and because there was no other way for them to defend themselves against this monster of ridicule, an immense laughter exploded wherever state power tried to look dignified—a vast Homeric laughter that swept all the nations with it.

I'll soon be going back to a country, many of whose citizens fail to appreciate their democratic rights and are surfeited with freedom. I shall tell them about your courage, about your stubborn persistence, your unbroken resistance—and also about your loneliness.

But before I go, I should like, in this place, to salute Giorgios Mangakis and Babis Protopappas. I salute them as representative of many, because along with many others they are twice deprived of freedom. My greetings are also a promise: I will not forget, I will not get used to it.

THE ARTIST'S FREEDOM OF
OPINION IN OUR SOCIETY

Address delivered June 29, 1973, in Florence.

Ladies and Gentlemen:

The Council of Europe and its Commission for Culture and Education are holding a symposium devoted to the far-reaching topic of freedom of opinion and the situation of the artist in our society. I thank you for asking me to participate. Quite rightly, you will expect to hear my opinion; but, much as the topic you have selected appeals to me personally, I must also speak in the name of those artists in Greece, as well as Czechoslovakia, whose freedom of opinion is restricted to the dimensions of a prison cell, and whose cold skepticism I seem to feel when it becomes necessary to discuss generally known facts in the pleasant atmosphere of this conference.

Since the task that has been set me is primarily· political, and since the artists of all European countries are placed willy-nilly in political contexts, I shall start by elucidating my own political position, which is not tied to any ideology.

After the Second World War, hence burdened with the guilt-ridden consequences of German political actions, I was forced, in the course of my work as a writer, to recognize that (if only marginally) the creative artist's supposed freedom is a fiction, that the artist not only sets his stamp on society and gives expression to his times, but is in equal measure a product of society and a child of the times—a spoiled child, a stepchild, an illegitimate child, or a ward of the state. I therefore took it for granted that along with my writing I would do the share of the political work that seemed to be incumbent on me as a citizen.

Artist and citizen? Isn't that a contradiction in terms? Is the anticivic role of the artist an ideological must? Or can a sociopolitical attitude, which declares the citizen to be an adult—and which is also my attitude—regard the artist as a being apart, to be tolerated and assigned a special preserve where he can disport himself like a nineteenth-century genius—lest the bourgeoisie be deprived of its thrills of terror?

Yes, I'm a writer and nevertheless a citizen. My political work has not been confined to the unrisky business of writing and signing resolutions. I have busied myself, often to the point of exhaustion, with the ups and downs of day-to-day politics. Smitten by no faith, inspired by no doctrine of salvation, I resolved after dispassionate study of the alternatives to support the Social Democratic Party. I decided in favor of the slow, parliamentary way, of the inalienable right to opposition, and acted on the knowledge that there is more than one truth and one reality, that several truths and realities, which are therefore relative, must compete with one another and tolerate one another.

Despite this liberal attitude, I became increasingly certain, in the years-long practice of my political sideline, that democratic socialism is the system most likely to win for mankind the increase in social justice and the legal guarantee of free and equal development, which have thus far been denied it by the prevailing systems of Western private capitalism and Eastern state capitalism. I have, further, become convinced that freedom in the arts is possible only where social and individual human rights are respected; wherever artists have to pay for relative freedom or a privileged status by rising above social conditions that tend to be latent abuses, they become an isolated elite, contenting themselves with the freedom of the playground. Their art, by befuddling or concealing, then becomes window dressing for a state of affairs that makes for servitude, and the artist becomes the whore of one power or another.

You have probably noticed that I, though favored with the privilege of speaking freely, have no intention of festooning the stereotype of the "free West" with decorative phrases. Conditions in Western Europe offer no justification for pointing an accusing finger at the artist's situation—the regimentation, the lack of freedom—in the Communist countries, while saying nothing of our own camp. Spain, Portugal, and Greece are governed by dictatorships. In those countries the torture of political adversaries is daily practice. But even in Western countries whose constitutions guarantee freedom of opinion, reality is at variance with the constitution. In France and Italy, television is controlled by the state; in the German Federal Republic, the Springer interests still dominate the newspaper market. In all European countries, moreover, economic power is able to influence the so-called independent press by according or withholding advertising. The concentration of capital and the monopoly status of the giant corporations are largely removed from democratic control, thus highlighting the impotence of freely elected parliaments.

The relative freedom or lack of freedom prevailing in democratically governed countries may be bearable, but it certainly does not justify self-righteous talk about Western freedom of opinion as opposed to the slavery prevailing in the East. For what is daily practice in the Eastern-bloc states, the regulation of art in accordance with party-line orthodoxy and the stupid subordination of the artist to the views of the bureaucracy, is at least a latent danger in the West. Moreover, as détente develops, the coexistence of ideologies and power structures will come about more quickly and with graver consequences in the economic field than in any other. In other words, Western private capitalism will start doing business with Communist state capitalism a lot more quickly than the issue of "free exchange of information" can be talked to death by working groups in Helsinki. For fear of endangering the big business of East-West trade, there will be a tendency to turn a blind eye in matters of "freedom of opinion." A Metternich sitting in all the deliberative bodies of the East and West may well try to promote an all-European order based on authoritarian states which, because periods of détente require peace and quiet, would tend to be police states.

The instrument of regulation is ready at hand. It is a demonstrable fact, and not without a certain comic interest, that when the word "humanism" is used and misused in the East and the West, ideological indoctrination becomes a way of divesting art and artists of the striving for diversity and the tendency to contradict. Regardless of whether it is the fundamental values of the Christian West or the pure doctrine of Communism that is once again in need of being defended against subversion, decadence, nihilism, etc., whether Solzhenitsyn is being punished in the Soviet Union or whether government grants to artists in France are subject to restrictive conditions—the word "humanism" is made to stand at attention and practice an intolerance that's as ugly as it is absurd.

Though "humus," "humane," and "humor" have the same root and hark back to life-giving moisture, the political application of humanism, that still-valid concept of the European Renaissance, demands that it be invoked whenever administrative humorlessness plants its dry-as-dust decrees in sandy soil. Not only the artists in the Eastern-bloc states, but we too in the West have reason to take fright or to raise protests seasoned with contempt when the word "humanism" is abused.

When George Orwell returned to England disillusioned from the Spanish Civil War, a good many writers, not to mention his publisher, ignored and boycotted him. The most infamous attacks on Alexander Solzhenitsyn were made by Soviet writers. The East German poet and singer Wolf Biermann is avoided like the plague by such opportunistic magnates of literature as Hermann Kant and Peter Hacks.* In his book *The New State and the Intellectuals,* Gottfried Benn proved once and for all that racism too can have a literary spokesman; and even the resentment of a Josef Goebbels against culture and intellectuals found its expression in articles that could not conceal the author's intellectual ability. Thanks to their intolerance, whole artistic movements, such as Italian futurism, were not only fellow travelers but actual pioneers of fascism.

In other words, popular as it is, the intellect-power antithesis doesn't hold water. Intellectuals have often been powerful enough to restrict freedom of opinion in the arts and to narrow it further in the realm of politics. And, on the other hand, democratic-minded politicians have often been obliged to impose tolerance on intolerantly warring artists and intellectuals, and to demand respect for freedom of opinion.

To enrich the confusion: the European Enlightenment, which in the eighteenth century gave birth to the ideas or concepts that still shape our lives—socialism, liberalism, and probably capitalism as well—also developed the notion of tolerance. And yet from the very start it demonstrated intolerance in clashes between its ideas. Anyone who is prepared to accept Michel de Montaigne as the father of the European Enlightenment may be amused to note how absurdly his descendants have reviled him as a reactionary or whipped him into line as an apostle of progress. Yet it cannot be denied that tolerance and intolerance, those twin scions of the early European Enlightenment, have been at war ever since—always in the jargon of the Enlightenment, sometimes with murderous outcome. Whether during the French Revolution the guillotine was made to serve progress and revolutionary virtue, or in the Soviet Union today undesirable artists and scientists are shut up in psychiatric hospitals, it has always been the lan-

---

*Establishment figures in the German Democratic Republic's Writers' Union, which expelled the satirical poet Biermann. —ED.

guage of the Enlightenment, with its appeal to freedom, that has cut back the human rights which are needed every day of our lives and, with a view to the perfect justice of the future, sown and perpetuated injustice.

I say all this without malice, just by way of dispelling illusions. For nowhere is it written that artists—or intellectuals, for that matter—are better, let alone more tolerant, than other citizens, endowed only with practical gifts. *Does he truly believe that?*

To argue from another direction: even if accounts in the *apparently* illustrated magazines show that Picasso was a wretched, hardhearted father, his portraits of children lose none of their expressiveness; whereas the bank clerk Meier's (or Dupont's) wretched taste in art need not detract from his pedagogic tolerance—or, in old-fashioned terms, from his warmhearted treatment of his children.

One need only read the pamphlets, or the exhibition catalogues and their prefaces, that transpose the quarrels between artistic trends into ideological gobbledygook, and compare them with the indoctrination pamphlets of parties claiming the exclusive right to rule, or the tracts of churches claiming exclusive possession of the truth. Though intolerance may not have its Esperanto, it has certainly developed its characteristic style.

To come out for freedom of opinion—and that's what I'm doing here—is to plead for diversity, to protect the desperately blasphemous outburst, to tolerate the kitsch that blooms everlastingly, to grant admittance at all times to subversive doubt, even where faith has established an entrenched society, to live with the contradictions characteristic of man and human society.

Since I'm not addressing some vaguely benevolent academy, but representatives of the Council of Europe, West European parliamentarians who bear political responsibility, I hope my plea for freedom of opinion won't just make you nod your heads; in some cases your opposition might be preferable. And because I'm not speaking to artists about the arts and their freedom—that is, confining myself to the intolerance of artists toward one another—I must now speak of political power and its abuse, a subject so vast that for fear of losing myself I shall concentrate on conditions in one West European and one East European country.

I am referring to the suppression of freedom of opinion under the Greek military dictatorship* and to the neo-Stalinist repression in Czechoslovakia following the intervention of the five Warsaw Pact powers.

You are aware that in Greece, as in Czechoslovakia, numerous artists, writers, journalists, and intellectuals have been imprisoned, along with many other citizens; that in Czechoslovakia they have been subjected to the vilest methods of interrogation and in Greece to torture. You are aware that in Czechoslovakia hundreds of artists and intellectuals are struggling to live without jobs or incomes. You have undoubtedly heard of the humiliating pressure put upon the students of Salonika and Athens. The methods of Stalinist and fascist terror are interchangeable; no ideological objective, no pragmatic motive—on the part of NATO or the Warsaw Pact, not to mention private-capitalist or state-capitalist big business—can justify their daily crimes. In Greece and Czechoslovakia the most repugnant aspects of the two bloc systems are revealed for all to see.

I'm not interested in rehashing familiar facts or in formulating cheap rhetorical pleas for freedom in Greece and Czechoslovakia. I wish only to entreat you to give a thought, in the Council of Europe but also at the Helsinki Conference, to the conditions prevailing in Greece and Czechoslovakia, and to use your political clout in an effort to remedy them.

The eruption of neo-Stalinism in Czechoslovakia has brought shame on the Eastern bloc, and the perpetuation of the military dictatorship in Greece involves the responsibility of Western Europe. The number of political prisoners in both blocs is incalculable. The security requirements of neither bloc

*Greece was ruled by the military from 1967 to 1974. —Ed.

can justify a relapse into Stalinist and fascist barbarism. Tolerance must not become a cynical exercise in which, for reasons of immediate interest, each ideological bloc tolerates the injustice in the other's camp and, since birds of a feather tend to be nice to one another, may go so far as to laud such tolerance as a triumph of détente. Injustice and the absence of freedom in the Eastern-bloc countries do not excuse the attitude of the Western democracies toward the Greek dictatorship.

Until you loudly and repeatedly—at home as parliamentarians and here in the Council of Europe—demand the restoration of democracy in Greece, Western Europe will only be partly justified in singing a democratic tune in Helsinki.

The man addressing you is someone who has always condemned the Cold War, its friend-and-foe ideology and its military consequences, and who has actively supported the policy of détente.

This policy has been pursued in spite of resistance, thus far successfully. It is based on treaties. Bastions that were manned only yesterday are today overgrown with weeds because they have become useless. Both blocs have thrown off ideological ballast. They are still distrustful of the new experiment. Insecure, because bereft of the enemy image, the two blocs confront each other armed to the teeth; they are constrained to coo détente, when they would prefer to rattle their sabers. So they shut their eyes to antagonisms. They look for the common denominator, for shared interests; they come to an understanding about mutual difficulties and start forming a united front against all those who take a skeptical, critical attitude toward the new consensus, which, because it is superficial, has a leveling effect in practice. For instance: the hard-boiled pragmatists and technocrats of both ideologically opposed technocracies note to their amazement that in both systems the exalted principle of all-out achievement is no longer held sacred, but is being systematically questioned, first and foremost by the younger generation—either coyly because of surfeit, or on the basis of political foresight, or on ethical grounds.

Defying the catechism of private as well as state capitalism, a generation that has grown to adulthood in peacetime is daring to question the doctrine of all-out achievement. Today we are beginning to hear from a generation which, as is often the case with younger generations, has not achieved anything and for that reason is shamelessly innocent. So much innocence is upsetting. Concerned and feeling persecuted, capitalist and Communist fathers are beginning to join forces. There is reason to fear that the very pillars of the state in both blocs, who only yesterday carried their mutual hatred to excess, are now agreed that the primary task of a détente policy must be to uphold the achievement principle, by drastic means if necessary.

A second example of a possible perversion of détente resulting from an alliance of the basically authoritarian and intolerant elements is as follows. In both blocs there are artists and intellectuals who in the fifties and sixties were persecuted in accordance with divergent ideological principles, for refusing to participate in the Cold War and advocating peaceful coexistence. But now that these pioneers think they have done their bit and gained for artists the right to meet freely and to exchange information and experience (after all, the Cold War is over; irreconcilable enemies have been metamorphosed into respected opponents)—now, I say, that private capitalists and Communist state capitalists are hobnobbing and concluding business deals, there are sobering indications that détente will take on a primarily big-business character, which will cast its shadow on cultural policy.

When—the foreign offices of the two blocs ask, with much head-shaking and not without a menacing undertone—when will these Solzhenitsyns and Bölls finally realize that the vital interests of the two détente-seeking blocs are exclusively economic, and that it's futile and harmful to détente to keep harping on the unavoidable consequences of normalization in Czechoslovakia and on military dictatorship in Greece, which must be tolerated for security reasons?

It is undemocratic, we are assured, to disregard the need of the working population in both blocs for job security, for increased exchange of consumer goods, for law and order, or, worse, to sacrifice all this to the needs of a hysterical minority, who still believe that freedom of opinion is the beginning and end of all things and knows no frontiers.

Have I exaggerated? I don't believe so; if anything, I have not gone far enough. My aim has been to keep the wounds of Prague and Athens open. You statesmen have it in your power to dispel the fears I have expressed.

Thank you for your attention.

THE DESTRUCTION OF MANKIND HAS BEGUN

Address delivered November 25, 1982, in Rome.

Chairman, Ladies and Gentlemen;

I shall try to express the thanks of all those who have been honored with the Antonio Feltrinelli Prize. This should be easy, since honors of this kind not only acknowledge work done, but are also encouragements to remain active in the future. Optimism is expressed at all award ceremonies, as though one could take it for granted that life will go on as it is. Up until now this attitude and pose have supported our concept of progress, for somehow life has gone on.

My message of thanks obtrudes doubt into traditional expectations. Our present makes the future questionable and in many respects unthinkable, for our present produces—since we have learned above all to produce—poverty, hunger, polluted air, polluted bodies of water, forests destroyed by acid rain or deforestation, arsenals that seem to pile up of their own accord and are capable of destroying mankind many times over.

Apart from its past and present historical significance, Rome, the city in which I am trying to give thanks, has come to be identified with the reports issued by the Club of Rome. These reports are our down-to-earth Revelation. We are not threatened by any judgment of the gods or of the one God. No Saint John is sitting on Patmos, penning obscure images of doom. No book of the seven seals has become our oracle. No, realistically and in the spirit of the times, we derive our vision from columns of figures assessing starvation; from the statistics of pauperization; from tables summarizing the ecological catastrophe—numbered madness, the apocalypse as balance sheet. The exact figures may be a matter for controversy, but the conclusion is inescapable that the destruction of mankind by man in a variety of ways has already begun.

On the assumption that scientists have also begun to question, if not to deny, the likelihood of a future as a field for further development, I hope to be speaking in the name of all the prize-winners if I now report briefly on my work as an author and call literature as well as myself into question.

Even more than the other arts, literature presupposes an assured field of action—that is, a future. It has outlived absolute rulers, theological and ideological dogmas, dictatorship after dictatorship; time and again censorships have been lifted and the word set free. The history of literature is in part a history of the victory of books over censorship, of writers over potentates. Thus, in the worst of times, literature has always been sure of one ally: the future. Silone and Moravia, Brecht and Döblin outlived fascism, just as Isaac Babel and Osip Mandelstam outlived Stalinism—though it killed them.

Literature has always had superior staying power. Sure of its aftereffect, it could count on time even if the echo to word and sentence, poem and thesis might take decades or even centuries to make itself heard. This advance payment, this provision of time, made the poorest writers rich. Even in the most loathsome times, these free spirits, whose growth rate went by the name of "immortality," were unconquerable; they could be imprisoned, executed, or driven into exile, as has been customary throughout the world down to our own day—but in the end the book won out and with it the word.

This was the case until today—or, rather, until yesterday. For with the loss of mankind's future, the "immortality" of literature, taken as a certainty until now, has ceased to be any-

138

thing more than wishful thinking. The book, formerly made to last forever, is beginning to resemble a nonreturnable bottle. It is not yet certain whether or not we still have a future, but already we have stopped reckoning with one. The same hubris that enables man to destroy himself is now threatening, before night falls, to darken the human spirit, to extinguish its dream of a better tomorrow and make a laughingstock of every utopia —including Ernst Bloch's *Hope Principle.*

A glance at the relation of forces in political and economic life shows that—against better knowledge—the overexploitation of natural resources is on the increase, that shameless justifications are offered for the pollution of air and water, that the potential for destruction of both superpowers and their satellites has long overstepped the threshold of madness. Despite all shouts of warning, no idea has managed to take on political reality. With all the display of force and with so many musclemen around, there is no force ready and willing to call a halt to already existing catastrophes and those that lie ahead. The holders of power engage in meaningless bustle and adjourn their responsibility from conference to conference.

All that remains is protest, enfeebled by abject fear, which soon, for want of words, will turn to speechless dread, because, in the face of the void, all sounds will have lost their meaning.

It may be, ladies and gentlemen, that my words of thanks frighten you and mar the sedately festive atmosphere to which this sort of day can reasonably lay claim. I suspect that my fellow prize-winners think my view of the situation unduly black, whereas they see it, at the worst, in tones of gray, since, after all, trite as it may sound, life does go on. New discoveries to be made, new inventions perfected, more and more books to be written. And I too, because I can't help it, shall persist in lining up words, in writing. Yet I know that the book I am planning to write can no longer pretend to certainty of the future. It will have to include a farewell to the damaged world, to wounded creatures, to us and our minds, which have thought of everything and of the end as well.

Everything that has thus far become a book for me has been subservient to time or has chafed under it. As a contemporary, I have written against the passage of time. The past made me throw it in the path of the present to make the present stumble. The future could only be understood on the basis of past made present. First and foremost, I found myself harnessed to German time, constrained to steer a course cutting obliquely across the epochs, disregarding the convenience of chronology. Epic moraines had to be cleared away, reality sloughed off again and again. There's no end to it. So many dead. And everywhere, even where life might release joy and pleasure might take its fling, the great crime casts its shadow, which time cannot efface.

Between books I have given politics what excess energy I could. Now and then something stirred. After all my experience with time and its contrary course, I inscribed a slow-moving animal in my escutcheon and said: Progress is a snail. At that time many wished—and so did I—that there could be jumping snails. Today I know, and recently wrote as much, that the snail is too quick for us. Already it has passed us by. But we, fallen out of nature, enemies of nature, still imagine that we're ahead of the snail.

Can human beings stop thinking about themselves? Are they —godlike creative beings endowed with reason, creators of more and more total inventions—capable of saying no to their inventions? Are they prepared to forgo the humanly possible and show some humility toward what's left of ruined nature? And lastly: have we the will to do what we can do—namely, feed one another until hunger ceases to be anything more than a legend, a once-upon-a-ghoulish-time story?

The answers to these questions are overdue. I myself have no answer, either. But in my perplexity I know that a future will only be possible again when we find an answer and do what, as guests on this orbiting chunk of nature, we owe to one another; namely, stop frightening one another, relieve one another of fear by disarming to the point of nakedness.

ON THE RIGHT TO RESIST

Address delivered January 30, 1983, at the Paulskirche (Saint Paul's Church) in Frankfurt.

I was five years old when Hitler and the National Socialists took power. I was thirty before I realized that my whole life—and my children's and their children's lives as well—would be blighted by the effects of that seizure of power. They will have to live with a divided country, with the limited sovereignty of two partial states, with enduring inherited guilt. You might call that unjust. Why should children and grandchildren have to suffer because of something that should long ago have been relegated to the history books, a lesson only half understood? Every nation feels justified in playing fast and loose with its history, in embellishing some events and suppressing others—why shouldn't we be entitled to embellish and suppress? Why can't the Germans, why shouldn't the Germans, succeed in living normally—that is, forgetfully?

There are many obvious reasons. I'll mention just one. Hitler's seizure of power—as we call it by way of simplification—was wanted and supported, opposed but not prevented by groups which still exist. All of them, though in varying degrees, are still burdened with responsibility for an irremediable breach in German history and for a criminal process without a parallel.

On the one hand, the big industrialists wanted Hitler, financed him, and hired his services; on the other hand, the unions could not resolve to call a general strike. For fear of the Reds, the bourgeoisie went over to the Brown Shirts. Timorously respectful of the democratic laws, the Social Democrats neglected to call for armed resistance and carry the unions with them. Both churches failed miserably; bowing to the new power, they forsook Christ and his message. As for the Communists, despite their antifascist rhetoric, their first obedience was to the Stalinist dogma that the Social Democrats were the main enemy. Hitler's power was consolidated not by his own strength, but by the weakness of his adversaries. Determination to resist was lacking.

Today there is a mass of literature supporting this and contrary theses. January 30, 1933, and its consequences have been analyzed by contemporaries and persons born later; some have called them a logical development, others an unfortunate accident. And since other horrible dates are in store for us, there will be no lack of clarifying as well as obfuscating literature. Perhaps we should console ourselves with the thought that the Germans are facing up to their history. How can we help it, since for every day in our lives history stands inescapably in our path.

Yet a residue subsists that cannot be clarified, that refuses to go away. Indeed, it seems to me that this residue grows with our distance from those events and that it cannot be defused. We are left with grief, with a constantly renewed dread of inadequately fenced-off abysses, and with the fear that we may again be faced with so fundamental a test and again fail.

At a time when in our day-to-day political life we are jolted by pressing problems, such as the economic crisis and unemployment, when it looks as though the future had nothing but catastrophes to offer, we are nevertheless as preoccupied with our past as if it had something to tell us, as if we owed it and it owed us an ultimate insight as terrifying as it is illuminating, as if without this insight we could not go on living in the present, not to speak of the future.

Before I try to put my finger on this insight, I must own to a certain skepticism, because German tradition shows how little the words of writers have counted, glad as their compatriots have been to use them as window dressing and even today to include them in political programs. Early in the Weimar Republic, leading writers warned us against the rising tide of barbarism, and published their insights, perforce in polemical terms. They went unheard, as they still do. Streets and squares and schools are named after them, yet Heinrich and Thomas Mann, Alfred Döblin and Bertolt Brecht are treated as émigrés, as foreigners. This is true in both German states.

We writers can stomach a good deal. Yet sometimes I feel nauseated and I'd like to drop out. If there were not—from Brandt to Vogel*—proof to the contrary, it would be impossible to go on. As it is, I shall continue my attempt to communicate the insight that fifty years ago, though clearly stated and sufficiently publicized, did not lead to decisive action. Today we are once again confronted with the question: When is resistance imperative? What sort of resistance does democracy not just admit of but demand for its protection? What danger to democracy makes resistance necessary? Does Article 20 of the constitution protect us against present dangers?†

Not that a new Hitler is clamoring for power. No such spinelessly accepted putsch is in the cards. The Federal Republic of Germany is not threatened by extremism of either the left or the right. And yet, though no Führer figure and no Party identifiable by its program have surfaced, a newly emerging danger is threatening to erode the substance of democratic government, though no date for a seizure of power has been announced.

Inveterate perfectionism, unlimited faith in technological progress, the government's excessive zeal in combating terror-

---

*Hans-Jochen Vogel, chairman of the German Social Democratic Party. —ED.
†Article 20, Paragraph 4, of the Constitution of the Federal Republic of Germany states: "All Germans shall have the right to resist any person or persons seeking to abolish [the] constitutional order, should no other remedy be possible." —ED.

ism, and a well-nigh-hysterical security-mindedness have opened the way to this danger. Block-by-block searches, data banks, listening devices, electronic identity cards—in short, the transparent society—these are the new ideology-free words that enrich George Orwell's Newspeak. Favored with democratic legitimacy, they not only foreshadow a police state, but also provide an advance sampling of its practice.

True, the new dangers have been recognized. Laws to protect privacy against the abuse of computerized information have been promulgated, and officials charged with enforcing them have been given full powers. But since the change of government in Bonn,* even this inadequate protection has shrunk to the point of absurdity. Security—that almighty justification for everything—has been given precedence over the citizen's right to lead his life.

All of us were taped and made "transparent" long ago. And those among you who in the last few years have found occasion to protest can be sure that your protest has been stored in word and image and is "retrievable." No demagogic tribunes of the people, no organized masses are preparing to suspend the democratic constitution, no one is planning to celebrate a new seizure of power with torchlight parades, no past disaster is likely to stage a repeat performance. No, the present threat is a new, soundless, foolproof system that purports to protect the citizen by encroaching on his rights, that claims to be fair on the ground that it spares no one, and that, with its uncontrolled ubiquity, may well protect democracy to death. In such a situation the Basic Law provides for the right to resist. Haste is in order, because it may soon be too late. True, "transparent democracy" doesn't function perfectly yet, but it's developing, with terrifying recklessness of late, now that our new government is in charge and the last liberal scruples have been removed along with his predecessor.

---

*The Social Democrats lost the 1982 election to the conservative CDU (Christian Democratic Union). —Ed.

That too is a seizure of power. A legal one, it goes without saying. Our schoolbooks tell us that. This is the law, law is order, so this is in order. If in doubt, consult the constitution, read the ambiguous Article 20 and its oracular Paragraph 4.

What, then, is to be done if "no other remedy" proves effectual? What sort of resistance can develop and be effective if for good reasons the use of force is excluded? Will the critical citizen content himself with being told that the state holds a monopoly on the use of force? Especially if he remembers that in 1933 the state held just such a monopoly?

Though reduced in its possibilities and liable to restitution for material damage, protest is still with us, as is the certainty that protesting citizens will be fed into the central computer. So better wait. And hope that the impending elections will provide some "other remedy." As democracy dies by its own hand, we are called upon to do it one last favor. Over and over again the assurance is given: we democrats stand firmly on the ground of our democratic constitution, although the nerves of both our feet tell us that this ground is being tunneled under—for security reasons, of course.

I say this has gone far enough. Those who are prepared to apply the insight conferred by January 30, 1933, to the crisis in our political life will no longer be able to content themselves with shuddering at the sight of democratically legitimized lawlessness. Not only the opposition, but all political parties are faced with a test. The unions as well as the churches are called upon to resist, and at the same time admonished to give a thought to their failure fifty years ago.

This year will be a year of harsh tests. This year—the year before Orwell's year—we shall see whether the German Federal Republic, unlike the Weimar Republic, can count on enough democrats—critical democrats and not appeasers, non-violent yet militant democrats, who are prepared to resist if need be. Confrontational situations lie ahead of us.

Thousands of tactical nuclear weapons are stationed in the Federal Republic. Chemical armaments including poison gases are stored here. From this it can be inferred that comparable arsenals are located in the German Democratic Republic. Already the two German states, with their dual dependency, are earmarked as a theater of nuclear warfare. The division of Germany and the limited sovereignty of both German states are among the lasting consequences of January 30, 1933. Each of the two states is an outpost of one or the other military bloc, and both states are confronted with the same certainty—namely, that even if "only" tactical nuclear weapons are employed, the end of the Germans is foreordained by the loyalty of both German states to a strategic pact. *Force majeure,* so to speak. The price that must be paid. The apologists of madness always have an explanation ready.

This too, I say, has gone far enough. We do not know whether the Geneva Conference can call a halt to the twofold madness. Already marked by failure, it holds out little hope. Moreover, the present West German government is too mindless and powerless to defend Germany's special interests against the allied superpower and our neighbor France. In place of a firm policy it offers cowardly toadying.

Thus, if in defiance of all reason medium-range missiles are deployed in Germany, only resistance can help. Resistance to objects that are no longer traditional armaments but instruments of genocide. For another lesson that must be drawn from January 30, 1933, is this: Hitler's legal seizure of power, which, being legal, was accepted without resistance, resulted in Auschwitz and in untold millions of dead. Of course, the crime for which we Germans bear responsibility cannot be compared to the nuclear genocide with which we are demonstrably threatened. But there is no great difference between the cynical disregard of the basic ethical values by the ill-famed Wannsee Conference, which decreed the "final solution," and the cynicism that in our own day produces war games simulating nuclear combat with projections of here fifty, there eighty million dead. Every German should know that we would be first to feed our numbers into the figuring machine. For whether we go by

the Eastern or by the Western figures, and however compla-
cently both sides protest that their intentions are purely defen-
sive, this sort of planning—unless worldwide resistance finally
puts an end to the strategy of calculated genocide—will result
in the last colossal work of man, the self-destruction of mankind.

January 30, 1933, confronts us with urgent questions, and
demands straightforward answers. What, in the light of our
constitution, does the demand for resistance mean? Already I
hear the outcries of our model democrats and smell the zeal of
our guardians of the constitution. Here is my answer: a people
that after fifty years is still suffering the consequences of its
failure to resist Hitler's seizure of power, a people that allowed
its democratic constitution to be expunged—legally and by majority vote—over the sole opposition (the Communist Party had
been outlawed) of the Social Democrats, a people marked by
such an experience ought to have learned to recognize different
but comparable dangers before it is too late and thus to look
upon the right to resist as a democratic imperative.

Never fear. I'm not advocating Molotov cocktails, plastic
bombs, and submachine guns. Civil disobedience, continuous,
imaginative protest, the churches' condemnation of the potential for genocide, and lastly a general strike—these are the possible forms of resistance I envisage.

I have tried to outline two absolutely inevitable developments. On the one hand, the Federal Republic of Germany is
submitting to the dictates of technocracy and becoming a police
state; on the other, it seems likely that the present parliamentary majority will consent to the stationing of medium-range
missiles on German soil and commit the Federal Republic to the
madness of the two superpowers—which amounts to nothing
less than calculated genocide. The two dangers may interlock
and exacerbate each other, for with the deployment of medium-
range missiles the police state's need for security would be
increased. The consequence would be total surveillance, prohibited zones, and "improvements" on the present German-

German frontier. I implore all those of you who hold positions of responsibility to consider that such a development will release counterviolence, desperate, mindless counterviolence. The dangers are not hidden or remote; at this very moment, we are in the process of catching up with Orwell's vision of 1984, if not surpassing it.

Enlightened resistance to this catastrophic development is discernible and growing. The worldwide peace movement has struck roots in Germany. In both German states it is above all the younger generation that is willing to take risks—great risks in the East, lesser ones in the West. Those who think it necessary to counter this nonviolent resistance with police violence are saddling the police with a task it should refuse. In the meantime, political leaders and bishops, representatives of the unions and of industry, scientists and artists, but also generals and high police officials have recognized the danger. Let us hope that they also recognize the democratic right to resist, lest the lesson of January 30 be in vain.

SUPERPOWER BACKYARDS

First published in Die Zeit, *October 1, 1982.*

Central America is the backyard of the United States. The
Mexican saying "My poor Mexico, how far you are from God,
and how close to the United States!" applies to these five small
republics. Nicaragua was our destination—"our" being myself,
Franz Alt, Johano Strasser, Ute Grass, the publisher Hermann
Schultz, and Dora Weidhaas, who served as the delegation's
interpreter. We came at the invitation of the Minister of Culture, the poet and priest Ernesto Cardenal, and of Sergio
Ramírez, also a writer and a member of the junta. We arrived
with no fixed ideas about Nicaragua, and we left, eight days
later, deeply changed.

My own knowledge of Nicaragua was drawn largely from
books. I was sympathetic to the revolution, but also skeptical.
What would twenty-one-year-old guerrilla commanders, fresh
from fighting in the jungles and the streets, know about running a country? How long would it be before this revolution
began to eat its children, as revolutions have done throughout
history? Spiritually as well as geographically, I felt closer to the
Solidarity movement in Poland.

Actually, as I see now, Solidarity and the Sandinistas have
much in common. Poland's fears of intervention by the Soviet
Union have their counterpart in Nicaragua's fears of intervention by the United States. In spite of the distance that separates

the two countries, they have similar relationships to the superpowers that dominate their parts of the world. The United
States seeks to undermine the Sandinistas and yet calls itself the
protector of Solidarity—and is seen as such by many misguided
people in Poland. The Soviet Union portrays itself as the protector of freedom movements in the Third World—and is mis-
takenly believed to be that by many Nicaraguans. In Nicaragua,
the misinformation spread by Tass, the Soviet news agency,
that Solidarity is counterrevolutionary is believed. Voice of
America broadcasts tell Poles that Nicaragua will soon be
firmly in the orbit of Cuba and the Soviet Union. And so the
covert "hate-the-Russians" sentiment in Poland corresponds to
the overt "hate-the-Yankees" opinion in Nicaragua.

I have visited both Poland and Nicaragua within the past
year, and I know how dangerous and stupid the two superpowers are as they go about dominating the countries in their backyards. But in the cases of Nicaragua and Poland, they will meet
strong resistance. It is a kind of resistance the superpowers
cannot understand, and it stems from the fact that the Solidarity
and Sandinista movements are both socialistic and Catholic.
More: they possess an early-Christian simplicity and directness
unlike the conventional forms of political power.

Even to a skeptic like me, the thought occurs that Rosa Luxemburg has appeared as the Virgin Mary to the Poles—and the
Holy Mother as Rosa Luxemburg to the Nicaraguans. These
two spontaneous movements mock the rigid Cold War ideology
of the Americans and the Central Committee Leninism of the
Russians. The revolution that was suppressed in Poland won in
Nicaragua three years ago, and it still survives and believes in
its future.

There are political prisoners in Nicaragua—former members of
Anastasio Somoza's National Guard, guilty of burning villages
and killing people. When we asked about them, Interior Minister Tomás Borge, who at fifty-two is an elder statesman of the

revolutionary government, immediately suggested that we visit Tipitapa prison.

Every prison is horrifying as an embodiment of the belief that people have the right to lock up their fellows, but Tipitapa is a far cry from Somoza's torture chambers. There is no capital punishment in Nicaragua, and the Sandinistas at least attempt to impose humane punishments. No other Third World country employs such methods, which are modeled after those used in Scandinavia.

There are several hundred former Guardsmen in Tipitapa prison. Some have been convicted of murder and torture. The prisoners work five days a week, building a hospital and two new wings with larger cells. Saturdays and Sundays are visiting days, and friends and relatives may come as often as they like and stay for three or four hours. There are special facilities for conjugal visits. When questioned by us, the inmates expressed their grievances freely—they complained about the shortage of quarters for conjugal visits, the lack of radios, the difficulty relatives in Managua and more distant villages have getting the fare to visit them.

Tomás Borge made himself available to hear the prisoners' questions and demands. He had spent five years in this prison and had experienced Somoza-style penology. He was kept in chains with a hood covering his head for nine months; he was tortured over a three-month span. It is customary for the victors of a revolution to take revenge on the survivors of the old order. But Borge does not believe in repaying injustice with injustice. "If we take revenge," he told us, "we will lose the victory of the revolution. Our revolution means renunciation of revenge."

"But didn't the revolutionary soldiers also pillage and torture out of revenge?" we asked. "Yes," Borge replied. "More than seven hundred Sandinistas have been imprisoned thus far for excesses like these. They plundered and tortured, and some of them even committed murder."

Convicted Sandinistas receive the same punishment as imprisoned National Guardsmen. Most of the Guardsmen fled, of course, in the wake of their defeat, and more than five thousand now operate along the border with Honduras, armed and supplied by the United States and reinforced by units trained in Miami. They conduct raids, burn down villages, and try to establish bases on Nicaraguan soil. Their aim is to incite a war between Nicaragua and Honduras, which could spread across all of Central America. If such a war broke out, President Reagan would bear the primary responsibility.

(On the flight to Managua, we had an unexpected layover in Miami. We rented a car and drove to two of the training camps for Cuban exiles and Somocistas south of Miami Beach. One of them was hidden behind mounds of garbage; the other was behind a fence with a metal sign on the gate reading "FBI Area." The penalty for unauthorized entry is ten years in prison and a ten-thousand-dollar fine.)

The U.S. government is not morally entitled to condemn the Soviet Union's aggression in Afghanistan or its pressure on Poland. Almost to the end it protected and bolstered with economic aid the murderous Somoza (and his father before him), and gave him guns and ammunition in the war against the Sandinistas. Now, in an attempt to destabilize the government, it has cut off all economic assistance and has halted the delivery of spare parts for U.S.-made equipment. And it is financing the Somocistas' guerrilla war against Nicaragua.

All this I knew before I made the trip, but in Nicaragua I saw it more clearly—and began to feel ashamed that the United States is an ally of my country. I wish West Germany would renounce that alliance—and not only because of American aggression against Nicaragua. The members of the Atlantic alliance are expected to accept quietly or even condone every action of their protector. America's aggressions, like those of the Soviet Union, have become pervasive, and they can no longer be excused as stupidity. Because I support both Solidarity and the Sandinistas I cannot remain indifferent to the wrongs done them by Russia and the United States.

How impoverished must a country be before it is not a threat to the U.S. government? Nicaragua has only 2.5 million people, most of them concentrated in Managua and a few towns. Somoza left an evil legacy: a looted treasury, a $1.6-billion foreign debt, and a capital city still bearing the scars of the 1972 earthquake (the money donated for reconstruction lined the pockets of the Somoza family). More than three hundred thousand people live in Managua's slums; Lake Managua has been turned into a cesspool; and the country's economic dependence is growing (last year exports totaled $500 million, and imports —of necessities only—totaled $850 million).

The prices that Nicaragua's main exports—coffee, cotton, sugar—fetch on the world market have fallen. Before the revolution, a hundred pounds of coffee brought $163; today they bring only $140. In sharp contrast, the prices of imported goods, from the simplest tools to farm machinery, have soared. Half of the country's staple foods—corn and beans—must be imported. The interest payments on loans from foreign banks add a crushing burden—and the loans are not nearly enough. Despite rising production, the country faces bankruptcy by 1985.

The Minister for Agrarian Reform, Jaime Wheelock, and the Minister for Interior Trade, Dionisio Marenco, briefed our group on economic matters. These two young men have been forced to acquire expertise in a hurry. They described the nation's economic goals in pragmatic terms, free from revolutionary rhetoric. Both praised the Sandinista "mixed economy," under which 20 percent of the land is owned by the state, 30 percent by the private sector, and 50 percent by cooperatives.

Wheelock took us on a tour of two cooperatives, which are located on land formerly owned by the Somoza family. The farmers had never owned land before. Five thousand peasants have received title to their own plots since the Sandinistas took power. We asked several farmers what was the biggest change the revolution had wrought in their lives, and their answers told us more about the necessity for the revolution than any party programs or theoretical arguments could. Before the revolution, they said, we worked hard yet we had nothing. Now we work harder—but the land is ours.

In nearly every farmer's hut hangs a picture of Augusto César Sandino, the farmer-general who is the father of the revolution. Beside it there is often a religious picture, usually of the Virgin Mary. To the poor—in Poland and in Nicaragua—religion provides emotional support and hope. In Nicaragua, the revolution has begun to redeem some of those hopes, but the people's religious faith remains strong. It has, however, become more down-to-earth, more secular, in the spirit of Catholic liberationist theology. Sandinistism is not opposed to Catholicism, and many priests work in the government. A new progressive Christianity is sweeping Latin America, and the Catholic hierarchy eyes it suspiciously or rejects it entirely. The Archbishop of Managua has been outspoken in his opposition to the Sandinistas. He threatens his parishioners with excommunication and foments strife within the church. His divisive actions have added to the country's problems. The Sandinista leadership has reacted to the Archbishop's provocations unwisely and oversensitively, which has made the situation worse. And a letter from Pope John Paul II to Nicaragua's bishops supporting the conservative clergy's antigovernment stand has exacerbated church-state tensions.

Polish Pope—Wojtyla! You are much traveled and sympathetic to the world's sufferings. Are the poor, the sick, and the persecuted still close to your heart, as you proved they were in Poland? Will you oppose the smug, the powerful, and the oppressors of the people—some of them cardinals and bishops in your own church? Will you understand that Sandinistism and Solidarity have common roots—though I admit that the people of Nicaragua and Poland are not aware of them yet?

Imagine that Lech Walesa and Ernesto Cardenal, the worker and the poet-priest, are sitting at your dinner table. They tell you of their peoples' anguish and hopes, their victories and defeats, their faults and shortcomings, their vulnerability and isolation, their worries about where their daily bread or corn-meal is coming from. What if—with the mysterious help of the Holy Spirit—you received an illumination? Could you then help Walesa and Cardenal recognize each other as brothers— and make them see you as their protector?

Like clumsy giants, the great powers confront each other. The long shadows they cast oppress the smaller nations around them. Look at them, Holy Father! The shadows fall not only on Poland but also on Nicaragua. If you fail to admonish the United States as you have so often admonished the Soviet Union, you too will be guilty if this small and poverty-racked country is torn apart by war and its revolution crushed. As I understand Christ's teachings, that revolution should be yours.

It is threatened, this revolution: from outside, and by economic weakness within—and also by the Sandinistas, whose glaring mistakes are seized upon by those who wish the revolution only failure. Fortunately, there are responsible individuals in the government who admit their mistakes. For example, after the relocation of Miskito Indians from fighting zones near the Honduran border to settlements in the interior, Daniel Ortega, co-ordinator of the junta, said: "We have made a multitude of mistakes. We knew nothing of their [the Indians'] religious culture, of ethnic peculiarities, almost nothing about their history or the problems of racism which the English and North American occupants left behind. Protestantism has always been the religion of the conquerors for Nicaragua. At this point the Somocistas in Honduras and Miami come in. They try to pull the Miskitos to their side and promise them independence, their own Miskito state. At the same time they attack the villages at the Honduran border and murder teachers and doctors."

From Managua we flew in a military helicopter to a newly built Miskito settlement. Roomy wood houses stand next to straw-covered temporary shelters; there is a health center and a large school barracks. Our escorts showed us how much the government has accomplished in a short time. Yet every resettlement—every forced uprooting of people—causes pain, no matter how well planned.

The soil, we are told, is better here than it is where the Indians previously lived. Eighty-five percent of the men, who formerly worked in mines, suffer from lung diseases. Now they receive medical care and pensions. Here, as elsewhere in the country, malaria has been stamped out. There is a compulsory immunization program. The American representative at the United Nations called the resettlement of the Miskitos "genocide." That is a lie, and it comes from a country that was founded on the stolen land and genocide of Indians.

We spoke with a young woman named Dora María Téllez, who had participated in the attack on Somoza's palace. She describes that battle today with little emotion. Heroism is a matter of necessity when people's troubles are great enough. Now she serves as vice-president of the State Council, and wants to expand its powers in the government. The country lacks strong political parties and election laws, and its constitution is obsolete. In 1985—so Tomás Borge, Sergio Ramírez, and Dora María Téllez assure us—Nicaragua's first election will be held. "Of course we will win!" they say, meaning the Sandinists. But they are too loud and too sure of themselves.

The Nicaraguans lack experience in democracy, sensitivity to constitutional rights, and knowledge of the necessity for sharing power. Perhaps the Dutch, the Germans, and the Scandinavians, all of them experienced in the day-to-day life of democracy, could offer the Sandinists cautious advice. A small, revolutionary country is at stake, and in need of a suitable constitution. Such help would not cost much. But to refuse to help or to offer only condescending advice could be a costly mistake.

When we arrived home, the contrast to Nicaragua was predictably obvious. Yet I was struck by a fresh view of my homeland —of its outward harshness and its inner banality. I saw a rich, well-equipped country whose society lacks cohesion—solidarity—even though it pretends to be a *Solidargemeinschaft* (solidarity community).

For months, there has been much controversy over the proposed *Ergänzungsabgabe* tax, under which salaried people would pay an additional 1 or 2 percent of their income so that the government could create new workplaces and additional apprentice positions. Nearly 2.5 million people in West Germany are out of work; many of them need education or training. But managers and employers with secure salaries—or, rather, their trade associations—have refused to make a gesture of solidarity. The main burden of the economic crisis must be borne by the workers. This officially condoned egoism mocks the concept of *Solidargemeinschaft* and signals the rise of a new class society.

Nicaragua needs help. Agriculture must be developed so that in time the country will be able to produce a surplus of beans and corn, which could help to counter the growing hunger all over the world. Will the government in Bonn understand (and why not?) that if we help Nicaragua we help ourselves? Or will it obey the wishes of the superpower-ally and get out the cudgel for Cuba—a familiar reaction which can club to death anything, not just the Sandinista revolution but also one's own thoughts?

When we arrived home, protest marches were being suppressed in Poland with water cannons and tear gas. Just when we thought it had been buried in the nineteenth century, the old-fashioned word "solidarity" seems fresh. I have seen it in Poland and in Nicaragua. In the backyards of the superpowers, solidarity is gaining strength, and peoples of other nations should feel neighborly toward it.